Appalachian Trail Guide to New York-New Jersey

NewYork-New Jersey Trail Conference

Eleventh Edition

Appalachian Trail Conference
Harpers Ferry

Appalachian Trail Guide to New York-New Jersey

Contents

Notice to All Trail Users

The information contained in this publication is the result of the best effort of the publisher, using information available to it at the time of printing. Changes resulting from maintenance work and relocations are constantly occurring and, therefore, no published route can be regarded as precisely accurate at the time you read this notice.

Notices of pending relocations are indicated. Maintenance of the Trail is conducted by volunteers and maintaining clubs listed in the guidebooks. Questions about the exact route of the Trail should be addressed to the Editor, *Appalachian Trail Guide to New York-New Jersey*, New York-New Jersey Trail Conference, G.P.O. Box 2250, New York, N.Y. 10116, (212) 685-9699. On the Trail, please pay close attention to—and follow—the white blazes and any direction signs.

Responsibility for Safety

It is extremely important to plan your hike, especially in places where water is scarce. Purify drinking water drawn from any source. Water purity cannot be guaranteed. The Appalachian Trail Conference and the various maintaining clubs attempt to locate good sources of water along the Trail but have no control over these sources and cannot, in any sense, be responsible for the quality of the water at any given time. You must determine the safety of all water you consume.

Certain risks are inherent in any Appalachian Trail hike. Each A.T. user must accept personal responsibility for his or her safety while on the Trail. The Appalachian Trail Conference and its member maintaining clubs cannot ensure the safety of any hiker on the Trail, and, when undertaking a hike on the Trail, each user thereby assumes the risk for any accident, illness, or injury that might occur on the Trail.

Enjoy your hike, but please take all appropriate precautions for your safety and well-being.

How to Use This Guide

The Trail data in this guide have been divided into 18 sections separated by highway crossings or other geographical features. The sections generally cover no more than a day's travel on the Trail. In addition, this guide includes a description of the southernmost Trail section in Connecticut, designated Connecticut Section Six. Part of that section passes through New York and is also designated New York Section 1. The northernmost Trail section entirely in New York is designated New York Section 2.

The data for each Trail section are divided into three or four parts. The first part includes general information needed primarily for planning. This material is arranged under individual headings in the following order:

Brief Description of Section
Road Approaches
Public Transportation
Maps
Shelters and Campsites
Supplies and Services
Public Accommodations

The detailed "Trail Description," the actual guide to the footpath, follows in two parts. Data are given first for walking south on the Trail and then for walking north. Trail data are presented in both directions of travel so hikers do not have to mentally reverse Trail descriptions. A column of distances on the left gives the mileage from the start of the section to important points along the Trail. Each point (such as stream crossings, shelters, summits, or important turns) is briefly described, followed by directions to the next point. In some of the sections, a fourth part, which gives information on important side trails, is also supplied. If many side trails cross the A.T. in a certain area, no attempt has been made to describe them all. Rather, the reader is referred to other publications that describe trails in the area in more detail.

Six maps, based on USGS topographic quadrangles with additional cartography by the NY-NJ TC, are included with this volume. In some sections, other available maps are also listed. It should be noted that, due to many recent relocations, the route of the A.T. is often shown incorrectly on unadjusted USGS topographic maps and on other commercially available maps.

The Appalachian Trail

The Appalachian Trail (A.T.) is a continuous, marked footpath extending 2,135 miles along the crest of the Appalachian mountain range from Katahdin, a granite monolith in the central Maine wilderness, south to Springer Mountain in Georgia.

The Trail traverses mostly public land in 14 states. Virginia has the longest section, with 552 miles, while West Virginia has the shortest, almost 26 miles along the Virginia-West Virginia boundary and a short swing into Harpers Ferry at the Maryland border. The highest elevation along the Trail is 6,643 feet at Clingmans Dome in the Great Smoky Mountains. The Trail is only slightly above sea level near its crossing of the Hudson River in New York.

Trail History

Credit for establishing the Trail belongs to three leaders and countless volunteers. The first proposal for the Trail to appear in print was an article by regional planner Benton MacKaye of Shirley, Massachusetts, entitled, "An Appalachian Trail, a Project in Regional Planning," in the October 1921 issue of the *Journal of the American Institute of Architects*. He envisioned a footpath along the Appalachian ridge line where urban people could retreat to nature.

MacKaye's challenge kindled considerable interest, but, at the time, most of the outdoor organizations that could participate in constructing such a trail were east of the Hudson River. Four existing trail systems could be incorporated into an A.T. The Appalachian Mountain Club (AMC) maintained an excellent series of trails in New England, but most ran north-south; the Trail could not cross New Hampshire until the chain of huts built and operated by the AMC permitted an east-west alignment. In Vermont, the southern 100 miles of the Long Trail, then being developed in the Green Mountains, were connected to the White Mountains by the trails of the Dartmouth Outing Club.

In 1923, a number of area hiking clubs that had formed the New York-New Jersey Trail Conference opened the first section of the A.T. in the Harriman-Bear Mountain section of Palisades Interstate Park.

The Appalachian Trail Conference (ATC) was formed in 1925 to stimulate greater interest in MacKaye's idea and coordinate the clubs' work in choosing and building the route. The Conference remains a nonprofit educational organization of volunteers dedicated to maintaining, managing, and protecting the Appalachian Trail.

Although interest in the Trail spread to Pennsylvania and New England, little further work was done until 1926, when Judge Arthur Perkins of Hartford, Connecticut, began persuading more groups to locate and cut the footpath through the wilderness. His enthusiasm provided the momentum that carried the Trail idea forward.

The southern states had had few trails and even fewer clubs. The "skyline" route followed by the A.T. in the south was developed largely within national forests. A number of clubs were formed in various parts of the southern Appalachians to take responsibility for the Trail there.

Judge Perkins, ATC chairman from 1927 to 1930, interested Myron H. Avery in the Trail. Avery, who chaired the Conference from 1931 to 1952, enlisted the aid and coordinated the work of hundreds of volunteers. The Trail was completed on August 14, 1937, when a Civilian Conservation Corps crew opened the last section (the ridge between Spaulding and Sugarloaf mountains in Maine).

At the eighth meeting of the ATC, in June 1937, Conference member Edward B. Ballard successfully proposed a plan for an "Appalachian Trailway" that would set apart a buffer on each side of the Trail, dedicated to the interests of those who travel on foot.

Steps taken to effect this long-range protection program culminated first in an October 15, 1938, agreement between the National Park Service and the U.S. Forest Service for the promotion of an Appalachian Trailway through the relevant national parks and forests, extending one mile on each side of the Trail. Within this zone, no new parallel roads would be built or any other incompatible development allowed. Timber cutting would not be permitted within 200 feet of the Trail. Similar agreements, creating a zone one-quarter-mile in width, were signed with most states through which the Trail passes.

After World War II, the encroachments of highways, housing developments, and summer resorts caused many relocations, and the problem of maintaining the Trail's wilderness character became more severe.

In 1968, Congress established a system of national scenic trails and designated the Appalachian Trail and the Pacific Crest Trail as the initial components. The National Trails System Act directs the secretary of the interior, in consultation with the secretary of agriculture, to administer the Appalachian Trail primarily as a footpath and protect the Trail against incompatible activities, including the use of motorized vehicles. Provision was also made for acquiring rights-of-way for the Trail, both inside and outside the boundaries of federally administered areas.

In 1970, supplemental agreements under the act—among the National Park Service, the U.S. Forest Service, and the Appalachian Trail Conference—established the specific responsibilities of these organizations for initial mapping, selection of rights-of-way, relocations, maintenance, development, acquisition of land, and protection of a permanent Trail. Agreements also were signed between the park service and the various states, encouraging them to acquire and protect a right-of-way for the Trail outside federal land.

Slow progress of federal efforts and lack of initiative by some states led Congress to strengthen the National Trails System Act. President Jimmy Carter signed the "Appalachian Trail amendment" on March 21, 1978.

The new legislation emphasized the need for protecting the Trail, including acquiring a corridor, and authorized $90 million for that purpose. With less than 140 miles unprotected by 1989, this part of the project is expected to be completed in the early 1990s.

Appalachian Trail Conference

In 1984, the Interior Department delegated the responsibility of managing the A.T. corridor lands to the Appalachian Trail Conference. The Conference and its clubs retain primary responsibility for maintaining the footpath, too.

The Conference publishes information on constructing and maintaining hiking trails, official A.T. guides, and information on hiking and trail use. Annual membership dues range from $18 to $30.

The Conference is governed by a volunteer Board of Managers, consisting of a chair, three vice chairs, a treasurer, a secretary, a corresponding secretary, and 18 members, six from each of the three regions of the Trail: New England, mid-Atlantic, and southern.

The Conference membership consists of organizations that maintain the Trail or contribute to the Trail project and individuals. ATC membership provides a subscription to *Appalachian Trailway News*, published five times a year, and 15-percent discounts on publications. The Conference also issues a newsletter, *The Register*, for Trail maintainers.

Membership forms and a complete list of publications are available from the Appalachian Trail Conference, P.O. Box 807, Harpers Ferry, W. Va. 25425, (304) 535-6331. The office is open nine a.m. to five p.m. (eastern time) Monday through Friday, and weekends from May through October.

The New York-New Jersey Trail Conference

The New York-New Jersey Trail Conference (NY-NJ TC) is a non-profit volunteer organization that maintains the Appalachian Trail from the Connecticut border to the Delaware Water Gap. In 1923, founders of the NY-NJ TC constructed and opened the first section of the A.T. in Bear Mountain-Harriman State Park, N.Y. Through a network of more than 70 local hiking clubs and more than 4,000 individual members, volunteers continue maintaining this section of the Trail as well as other trails in New York and New Jersey.

The NY-NJ TC was formed in 1920 when local hiking clubs gathered to plan a system of marked trails to make Bear Mountain-Harriman State Park more accessible to the public. During the 1930s, more trails were built, and a system of trail maintenance was developed, giving each hiking club a share of the responsibility. Today, this network covers nearly 800 miles of marked trails.

In addition to maintaining the A.T. in New York and New Jersey, the NY-NJ TC is responsible for relocating the Trail away from roads and unprotected private lands and onto protected woodlands. Of the more than 160 miles of the Trail in New York and New Jersey, 55 miles have been relocated into a protected corridor approximately

1,000 feet wide. The NY-NJ TC and state and federal officials are designing cooperative agreements and local management plans for the Trail that will define the obligations and responsibilities of all parties. The relocations in these two states are making the A.T. through New York and New Jersey a hike you won't want to miss.

In addition to trail-building and maintenance, NY-NJ TC volunteers devote many hours to other projects and issues affecting the trails. Every spring, the Conference sponsors "Litter Day," a massive effort to clean trash out of our woods. The Conference also supports the enactment and implementation of "bottle bills" to reduce litter along the trails. In addition, the Conference protects woodlands, wildlife, and places of scenic beauty. For example, the Conference is working with other environmental groups to prevent major development in Sterling Forest in New York that would destroy the natural beauty of the area.

For further information, write or call the New York-New Jersey Trail Conference, G.P.O. Box 2250, New York, N.Y. 10116, (212) 685-9699.

The Route of the Appalachian Trail in New York and New Jersey

The Appalachian Trail crosses the Connecticut-New York state line at Hoyt Road. It passes through Fahnestock State Park and continues southwest to the Bear Mountain Bridge.

After crossing the Hudson River, the Trail direction is west for southbound hikers and east for northbound hikers. In Harriman State Park, the Trail uses a portion of the original route established in 1923 and then follows the ridges of Bellvale and Bearfort mountains west of Greenwood Lake, where it enters New Jersey.

Following a newly constructed route on a protected corridor acquired by the State of New Jersey, the A.T. runs nearly parallel to the state line until it reaches High Point State Park, where it turns nearly southward and continues into Stokes State Forest. From here to the Delaware River, it generally follows the ridge line of the Kittatinny Mountains, sometimes on state land and sometimes through the Delaware Water Gap National Recreation Area. It crosses the Delaware River on the I-80 toll bridge at the gap.

Use of the Trail

Trail Marking

The Appalachian Trail is marked for travel in both directions. The marks are white-paint blazes about two inches wide and six inches high on trees, posts, and rocks. Occasionally, on open ledges, stone cairns identify the route. In some areas, diamond-shaped A.T. metal markers mark the Trail. Two blazes, one above the other, signal an obscure turn, a change in route, or a warning to check blazes carefully. In New York and New Jersey, the upper of the two blazes indicating a turn is offset in the direction of the turn.

When the route is not obvious, normal marking procedure is to position the blazes so that anyone standing at one blaze will always be able to see the next. When the footway is unmistakable, blazes frequently are farther apart. If you have gone a quarter-mile without seeing a blaze, retrace your steps until you locate one and then check to ensure that you did not miss a turn. Since the Trail is marked for both directions, a glance back may locate blazes for travel in the opposite direction.

Side trails from the A.T. to water, viewpoints, and shelters usually are blazed in blue paint. Intersecting trails not part of the A.T. are blazed in a variety of colors.

At trail junctions or near important features, the Trail route is sometimes marked by signs, too. Some list mileages and include detailed information.

Trail Relocations

Always follow the marked Trail. If it differs from the guidebook's Trail description, it is because the Trail was recently relocated in the area, probably to avoid a hazard or undesirable feature or to remove it from private property. If you use the old Trail, you may be trespassing, as well as generating ill will toward the Trail community.

Information on relocations may be obtained by consulting the bi-monthly *Trail Walker*, published by the New York-New Jersey Trail Conference, or *Appalachian Trailway News*, published by the Appalachian Trail Conference five times a year. Every effort has been made in this guide to alert you to relocations that may occur. Do not follow new trails that are not blazed, because they may not be open to the public yet.

Water

In many areas, water sources along the Trail are unsafe for drinking, and a considerable distance may pass before potable water can be obtained. Carrying a canteen is necessary; a one-quart canteen may not be enough, especially in dry seasons. The exertion of hiking, combined with water shortages, could lead to dehydration, increasing fatigue and marring an otherwise enjoyable experience.

Although the A.T. may have sources of clean, potable water, any water source can become polluted. Most water sources along the Trail are unprotected and consequently very susceptible to contamination. All water should be purified by boiling, chemical treatment, or portable water filters before using. Take particular care to protect the purity of all water sources. Never wash dishes, clothes, or hands in the water source. Make sure food and human wastes are buried well away from any water source.

Equipment

The basic equipment rule is, never carry more than you need.

Some items should be with you on every hike: this guidebook or the *A.T. Data Book*; maps; canteen; flashlight, even on day trips; whistle; emergency food; tissues; matches and fire starter; multipurpose knife; compass; rain gear; proper shoes and socks; warm, dry, spare clothes; and a first-aid kit (see page 20).

Take the time to consult periodicals, books, employees of outfitter stores, and other hikers before choosing the equipment that is best for you.

Navigation

The compass variation, or declination, in New York and New Jersey varies from 13 degrees at the Connecticut-New York line to 11 degrees at the New Jersey-Pennsylvania line. This means that true north varies from 11 to 13 degrees to the right of the direction indicated by the compass needle, depending upon the location of the hiker. This is a significant variation that should be taken into account when the hiker orients himself or his map. The approximate compass declination at different points along the Trail is shown on each map accompanying this guide. Due to iron deposits in the area immediately west of the Hudson River (New York Sections Ten to Thirteen and New Jersey Section One), compass readings in this area may not be dependable.

Getting Lost

Stop, if you have walked more than a quarter-mile (1,320 feet, or roughly five minutes of hiking) without noticing a blaze or other Trail indicator (see page six). If you find no indication of the Trail, retrace your course until one appears. The cardinal mistake behind unfortunate experiences is insisting on continuing when the route seems obscure or dubious. Haste, even in a desire to reach camp before dark, only complicates the difficulty. When in doubt, remain where you are, to avoid straying farther from the route.

Hiking long distances alone should be avoided, but if undertaken, it requires extra precautions. A lone hiker who suffers a serious accident or illness might be risking death if he has not planned for the remote chance of isolation. Your destinations and estimated times of arrival should be known to someone who will initiate inquiries or a search if you do not appear when expected. On long trips, reporting your plans and progress every few days is a wise precaution.

A lone hiker who loses his way and chooses to bushwhack toward town runs considerable risks if an accident occurs. If he falls helpless away from a used trail, he might not be discovered for days or even weeks. Lone hikers are advised to stay on the Trail (or at least on a trail), even if it means spending an unplanned night in the woods in sight of a distant electric light. Your pack should always contain enough food, water, and protective clothing to sustain you until daylight, when a careful retracing of your steps might lead you back to a safe route.

Distress Signals

An emergency call for distress consists of three short calls, audible or visible, repeated at regular intervals. A whistle is particularly good for audible signals. Visible signals may include, in daytime, light flashed with a mirror or smoke puffs; at night, a flashlight or three small bright fires.

Anyone recognizing such a signal should acknowledge with two calls—if possible, by the same method—then go to the distressed and determine the nature of the emergency. Arrange for more aid, if necessary.

Most of the A.T. is used enough that, if you are injured, you can expect to be found. However, if an area is remote and the weather bad, fewer hikers will be on the Trail. In this case, it might be best to study the guidebook or map for the nearest place people are likely to be and attempt to move in that direction. If it is necessary to leave a heavy pack behind, be sure to take essentials, in case your rescue is delayed. In bad weather, a night in the open without proper covering could be dangerous.

Publications

NY-NJ TC publications include the *New York Walk Book*, *Day Walker*, *Guide to the Long Path*, *Circuit Hikes in Northern New Jersey*, and maps for Bear Mountain-Harriman State Park, North Jersey trails, East Hudson trails, South Taconic trails, Kittatinny trails, West Hudson trails, the Shawangunks, and the Catskills. The first five of these map sets cover sections of the A.T. The NY-NJ TC also publishes the *Trail Walker*, a bimonthly newspaper for members, that includes information on A.T. relocations in the two states. Members also receive a publications discount. For further information, write or call the New York-New Jersey Trail Conference, G.P.O. Box 2250, New York, N.Y. 10116, (212) 685-9699.

The Appalachian Trail Conference, as part of its charter to serve as a clearinghouse of information on the Trail, publishes a number of books other than guides and also sells books from other publishers. ATC members receive a 15-percent discount on publications sold through the Conference. Proceeds from sales help underwrite the costs of A.T. maintenance and Trail-corridor management.

A complete list of the publications and merchandise available from ATC can be obtained by writing ATC at P.O. Box 807, Harpers Ferry, W. Va. 25425, or calling (304) 535-6331.

Those seeking basic information about hiking and equipment might consider joining one of the hiking clubs connected with ATC or consult the following books:

The Complete Walker III, by Colin Fletcher, Alfred A. Knopf, New York, 1987.

Backpacking One Step at a Time, by Harvey Manning, Vintage Books, New York, 1986.

Maps and Compasses: A User's Handbook, by Percy W. Blandford, TAB Books, Inc., Blue Ridge Summit, Pa., 1984

First Aid along the Trail
by Robert Ohler, M.D.

Hikers encounter a wide variety of terrain and climatic conditions along the Appalachian Trail. Prepare for the possibility of injuries. Some of the more common Trail-related medical problems are briefly discussed below.

Preparation is key to a safe trip. If possible, every hiker should take the free courses in advanced first aid and cardiopulmonary-resuscitation (CPR) techniques offered in most communities by the American Red Cross.

Even without this training, you can be prepared for accidents. Emergency situations can develop. Analyses of serious accidents have shown that a substantial number originate at home, in the planning stage of the trip.

Think about communications. Have you informed your relatives and friends about your expedition: locations, schedule, and time of return? Has all of your equipment been carefully checked? Considering the season and altitude, have you provided for water, food, and shelter?

While hiking, set your own comfortable pace. If you are injured or lost or a storm strikes, stop. Remember, your brain is your most important survival tool. Inattention can start a chain of events leading to disaster.

If an accident occurs, treat the injury first. If outside help is needed, at least one person should stay with the injured hiker. Two people should go for help and carry with them notes on the exact location of the accident, what has been done to aid the injured, and what help is needed. The injured will need encouragement, assurances of help, and confidence in your competence. Treat him gently. Keep him supine, warm, and quiet. Protect him from the weather with insulation below and above him. Examine him carefully, noting all possible injuries.

General Emergencies

Back or neck injuries: Immobilize the victim's entire body, where he lies. Protect head and neck from movement if the neck is injured, and treat as a fracture. Transportation must be on a rigid frame, such as a litter or a door. The spinal cord could be severed by inexpert handling. This type of injury must be handled by a large group of experienced personnel. Obtain outside help.

Bleeding: Stop the flow of blood by using a method appropriate to the amount and type of bleeding. Exerting pressure over the wound with the fingers, with or without a dressing, may be sufficient. Minor arterial bleeding can be controlled with local pressure and bandaging. Major arterial bleeding might require compressing an artery against a bone to stop the flow of blood. Elevate the arm or legs above the heart. To stop bleeding from an artery in the leg, place a hand in the groin and press toward the inside of the leg. Stop arterial bleeding from an arm by placing a hand between the armpit and elbow and pressing toward the inside of the arm.

Apply a tourniquet only if you are unable to control severe bleeding by pressure and elevation. *Warning: This method should be used only when the limb will be lost anyway.* Once applied, a tourniquet should only be removed by medical personnel equipped to stop the bleeding by other means and to restore lost blood. The tourniquet should be located between the wound and the heart. If there is a traumatic amputation (loss of hand, leg, or foot), place the tourniquet two inches above the amputation.

Wind Chill Chart

Actual Temperature
(°F)

		50	40	30	20	10	0	−10	−20	−30	−40	−50
		Equivalent Temperature										
		(°F)										
	0	50	40	30	20	10	0	−10	−20	−30	−40	−50
	5	48	37	27	16	6	−5	−15	−26	−36	−47	−57
	10	40	28	16	4	−9	−21	−33	−46	−58	−70	−83
	15	36	22	9	−5	−18	−36	−45	−58	−72	−85	−99
	20	32	18	4	−10	−25	−39	−53	−67	−82	−96	−110
	25	30	16	0	−15	−29	−44	−59	−74	−88	−104	−118
	30	28	13	−2	−18	−33	−48	−63	−79	−94	−109	−125
	35	27	11	−4	−20	−35	−49	−67	−82	−98	−113	−129
	40	26	10	−6	−21	−37	−53	−69	−85	−100	−116	−132

Wind Speed (mph)

This chart illustrates the important relationship between wind and temperature.

Blisters: Good boot fit, without points of irritation or pressure, should be proven before a hike. Always keep feet dry while hiking. Prevent blisters by responding early to any discomfort. Place adhesive tape or moleskin over areas of developing redness or soreness. If irritation can be relieved, allow blister fluid to be reabsorbed. If a blister forms and continued irritation makes draining it necessary, wash the area with soap and water and prick the edge of the blister with a needle that has been sterilized by the flame of a match. Bandage with a sterile gauze pad and moleskin.

Dislocation of a leg or arm joint is extremely painful. Do not try to put it back in place. Immobilize the entire limb with splints in the position it is found.

Exhaustion is caused by inadequate food consumption, dehydration and salt deficiency, overexertion, or all three. The victim may lose motivation, slow down, gasp for air, complain of weakness, dizziness, nausea, or headache. Treat by feeding, especially carbohydrates. Slowly replace lost water (normal fluid intake should be two to four quarts per day). Give salt dissolved in water (one teaspoon per cup). In the case of overexertion, rest is essential.

Fractures of legs, ankles, or arms must be splinted before moving the victim. After treating wounds, use any available material that will offer firm support, such as tree branches or boards. Pad each side of the arm or leg with soft material, supporting and immobilizing the joints above and below the injury. Bind the splints together with strips of cloth.

Shock should be expected after all injuries. It is a potentially fatal depression of body functions that is made more critical with improper handling, cold, fatigue, and anxiety. Relieve the pain as quickly as possible. Do not administer aspirin if severe bleeding is present; Tylenol or other nonaspirin pain relievers are safe to give.

Look for nausea, paleness, trembling, sweating, or thirst. Lay the hiker flat on his back, and raise his feet slightly, or position him, if he can be safely moved, so his head is down the slope. Protect him from the wind, and keep him as warm as possible. A campfire will help.

Sprains: Look or feel for soreness or swelling. Bandage, and treat as a fracture. Cool and raise joint.

Wounds (except eye wounds) should be cleaned with soap and water. If possible, apply a clean dressing to protect the wound from further contamination.

Chilling and Freezing Emergencies

Every hiker should be familiar with the symptoms, treatment, and methods of preventing the common and sometimes fatal condition of *hypothermia*. Wind chill and/or body wetness, particularly aggravated by fatigue and hunger, can rapidly drain body heat to dangerously low levels. This often occurs at temperatures well above freezing. Shivering, lethargy, mental slowing, and confusion are early symptoms of hypothermia, which can begin without the victim's realizing it and, if untreated, can lead to death.

Always keep dry spare clothing and a water-repellent windbreaker in your pack, and wear a hat in chilling weather. Wet clothing loses much of its insulating value, although wet wool is warmer than other wet fabrics. Always, when in chilling conditions, suspect the onset of hypothermia.

To treat this potentially fatal condition, immediately seek shelter, and warm the entire body, preferably by placing it in a sleeping bag and administering warm liquids. The addition of another person's body heat may aid in warming.

A sign of frostbite is grayish or waxy, yellow-white spots on the skin. The frozen area will be numb. To thaw, warm the frozen part by direct contact with bare flesh. When first frozen, a cheek, nose, or chin can often be thawed by covering with a hand taken from a warm glove. Superficially frostbitten hands sometimes can be thawed by placing them under armpits, on the stomach, or between the thighs. With a partner, feet can be treated similarly. Do not rub frozen flesh.

Frozen, deeper layers of tissue beneath the skin are characterized by a solid, "woody" feeling and an inability to move the flesh over bony prominences. Tissue loss is minimized by rapid rewarming of the area in water slightly below 105 degrees Fahrenheit (measure accurately with a thermometer).

Thawing of a frozen foot should not be attempted until the patient has been evacuated to a place where rapid, controlled thawing can take place. Walking on a frozen foot is entirely possible and does not cause increased damage. Walking after thawing is impossible.

Never rewarm over a stove or fire. This "cooks" flesh and results in extensive loss of tissue.

Treatment of a deep freezing injury after rewarming must be done in a hospital.

Heat Emergencies

Exposure to extremely high temperatures, high humidity, and direct sunlight can cause health problems.

Heat cramps are usually caused by strenuous activity in high heat and humidity, when sweating depletes salt levels in blood and tissues. Symptoms are intermittent cramps in legs and abdominal wall and painful spasms of muscles. Pupils of eyes may dilate with each spasm. The skin becomes cold and clammy. Treat with rest and salt dissolved in water (one teaspoon of salt per glass).

Heat exhaustion, caused by physical exercise during prolonged exposure to heat, is a breakdown of the body's heat-regulating system. The circulatory system is disrupted, reducing the supply of blood to vital organs such as the brain, heart, and lungs. The victim can have heat cramps and sweat heavily. Skin is moist and cold with face flushed, then pale. Pulse can be unsteady and blood pressure low. He may vomit and be delirious. Place the victim in shade, flat on his back, with feet 8-12 inches higher than head. Give him sips of salt water—half a glass every 15 minutes—for about an hour. Loosen his clothes. Apply cold cloths.

Heat stroke and *sun stroke* are caused by the failure of the heat-regulating system to cool the body by sweating. They are life-threatening emergencies. Body temperature can rise to 106 degrees or higher. Symptoms include weakness, nausea, headache, heat cramps, exhaustion, body temperature rising rapidly, pounding pulse, and high blood pressure. The victim may be delirious or comatose. Sweating will stop before heat stroke becomes apparent. Armpits may be dry and skin flushed and pink, turning ashen or purple in later stages. Move victim to cool place immediately. Cool the body in any way possible (*e.g.* sponging). Body temperature must be regulated artificially from outside of the body until the heat-regulating system can be rebalanced. Be careful not to overchill once temperature goes below 102 degrees.

Heat weakness: Symptoms are fatigue, headache, mental and physical inefficiency, heavy sweating, high pulse rate, and general weakness. Drink plenty of water, find as cool a spot as possible, keep quiet, and replenish salt loss.

Sunburn causes redness of the skin, discoloration, swelling, and pain. It occurs rapidly and can be severe at higher elevations. It can be prevented by applying a commercial sun screen; zinc oxide is the most effective. Treat by protecting from further exposure and covering the area with ointment and a dressing. Give the victim large amounts of fluids.

Artificial Respiration

Artificial respiration might be required when an obstruction constricts the air passages or after respiratory failure caused by air being depleted of oxygen, such as after electrocution, by drowning, or toxic gases in the air. Quick action is necessary if the victim's lips, fingernail beds, or tongue have become blue, if he is unconscious, or if the pupils of his eyes become enlarged. If food or a foreign body is lodged in the air passage and coughing is ineffective, try to remove it with the fingers. If the foreign body is inaccessible, grasp the victim from behind. With one hand, hold the opposite wrist just below the breastbone. Squeeze rapidly and firmly, expelling air forcibly from the lungs, to expel the foreign body. Repeat this maneuver two to three times, if necessary.

If breathing stops, administer artificial respiration, as air may be forced around the obstruction into the lungs. The mouth-to-mouth, or mouth-to-nose, method of forcing air into the victim's lungs should be used. The preferred method is:

1. Clear the victim's mouth of any obstructions.
2. Place one hand under the victim's neck and lift.
3. Place heel of other hand on the forehead, and tilt head backwards. (Maintain this position during procedure.) Use thumb and index finger to pinch nostrils.
4. Open your mouth, and make a seal with it over victim's mouth. If the victim is a small child, cover both the nose and the mouth.
5. Breathe deeply, and blow out about every five seconds, or 12 breaths a minute.
6. Watch victim's chest for expansion.
7. Listen for exhalation.

Poison Ivy

Poison ivy is the only plant commonly found along the Trail that irritates the skin. It is most often found as a vine trailing near the ground or climbing on fences or trees, sometimes up to 20 feet from the ground. A less common variety that is often unrecognized is an erect shrub, standing alone and unsupported, up to 10 feet tall.

The leaves are in clusters of three, the end leaf with a longer stalk and pointed tip, light green in spring but darkening as the weeks pass. The inconspicuous flowers are greenish; the berries, white or cream. The irritating oil is in all parts of the plant, even in dead plants, and is carried in the smoke of burning plants. Those who believe themselves immune may find that they are seriously suscep-tible if the concentration is great enough or the toxins are ingested.

If you have touched poison ivy, wash immediately with strong soap (but not with one containing added oil). If a rash develops in the next day or so, treat it with calamine lotion or Solarcaine. Do not scratch. If blisters become serious or the rash spreads to the eyes, see a doctor.

Lyme Disease

Lyme disease is contracted from bites of certain infected ticks. Hikers should be aware of the symptoms and monitor themselves and their partners for signs of the disease. When treated early, Lyme disease usually can be cured with antibiotics.

Inspect yourself for ticks and tick bites at the end of each day. The four types of ticks known to spread Lyme disease are smaller than the dog tick, about the size of a pin head, and not easily seen. They are often called "deer ticks" because they feed on deer, a host for the disease.

The early signs of a tick bite infected with Lyme disease are a red spot with a white center that enlarges and spreads, severe fatigue, chills, headaches, muscle aches, fever, malaise, and a stiff neck. However, one-quarter of all people with an infected tick bite show none of the early symptons.

Later effects of the disease, which may not appear for months or years, are severe fatigue, dizziness, shortness of breath, cardiac irregularities, memory and concentration problems, facial paralysis, meningitis, shooting pains in the arms and legs, and other symptoms resembling multiple sclerosis, brain tumors, stroke, alcoholism, mental depression, Alzheimer's disease, and anorexia nervosa.

Some doctors are not yet well-informed about the disease and can misdiagnose the symptoms. It may be necessary to contact a university medical center or other research center if you suspect you have been bitten by an infected tick.

It is not believed people can build a lasting immunity to Lyme disease. A hiker who has contracted and been treated for the disease should still take precautions.

Lightning Strikes

Although the odds of being struck by lightning are low, 200 to 400 people a year are killed by lightning in the United States. Respect the force of lightning, and seek shelter during a storm.

Do not start a hike if thunderstorms are likely. If caught in a storm, immediately find shelter. Hard-roofed automobiles or large buildings are best; tents and convertible automobiles offer no protection. When indoors, stay away from windows, open doors, fireplaces, and large metal objects. Do not hold a potential lightning rod, such as a fishing pole. Avoid tall structures, such as ski lifts, flagpoles, powerline towers, and the tallest trees or hilltops. If you cannot enter a building or car, take shelter in a stand of smaller trees. Avoid clearings. If caught in the open, crouch down, or roll into a ball. If you are in water, get out. Spread out groups, so that everyone is not struck by a single bolt.

If a person is struck by lightning or splashed by a charge hitting a nearby object, the victim will probably be thrown, perhaps a great distance. Clothes can be burned or torn. Metal objects (such as belt buckles) may be hot. The victim often has severe muscle contractions (which can cause breathing difficulties), confusion, and temporary blindness or deafness. In more severe cases, the victim may have feathered or sunburst patterns of burns over the skin or ruptured eardrums. He may lose consciousness or breathe irregularly. Occasionally, victims stop breathing and suffer cardiac arrest.

If someone is struck by lightning, perform artificial respiration (see page 16) and CPR until emergency technicians arrive or you can transport the injured to a hospital. Lightning victims may be unable to breathe independently for 15 to 30 minutes but can recover quickly once they can breathe on their own. Do not give up early; a seemingly lifeless individual can be saved if you breathe for him promptly after the strike.

If you come across someone who appears to have been struck, assume that the victim was thrown a great distance, protect the spine, treat other injuries, then transport him to the hospital.

Snakebites

Hikers on the Appalachian Trail may encounter copperheads, timber rattlesnakes, or cottonmouths (water moccasins). These are pit vipers, characterized by triangular heads, vertical elliptical pupils, two or fewer hinged fangs on the front part of the jaw (fangs are replaced every six to ten weeks), heat-sensory facial pits on the sides of the head and a single row of scales on the underbelly by the tail. Rattlesnakes have rattles on the tail.

The best way to avoid being bitten by poisonous snakes is to avoid their known habitats and reaching into dark areas (use a walking stick to move suspicious objects). Wear protective clothing, especially on feet and lower legs. Do not hike alone or at night in snake territory; always have a flashlight and walking stick. Do not handle snakes. A snake can bite and envenomate you with a reflex action for 20 to 60 minutes after its death.

Not all snakebites result in envenomation, even if the snake is poisonous. The signs of envenomation are one or more fang marks in addition to rows of teeth marks, burning pain, and swelling at the bite (swelling usually begins within five to ten minutes of envenomation and can become very severe). Lips, face, and scalp may tingle and become numb 30 to 60 minutes after the bite. (If these symptoms are immediate and the victim is frightened and excited, then they are most likely due to hyperventilation.) Thirty to 90 minutes after the bite, the victim's eyes and mouth may twitch, and he may have a rubbery or metallic taste in his mouth. He may sweat, experience weakness, nausea and vomiting, or faint one to two hours after the bite. Bruising at the bite usually begins within two to three hours, and large blood blisters may develop within six to ten hours. The victim may have difficulty breathing, have bloody urine and vomit blood, and may collapse six to 12 hours after the bite.

If someone you are with has been bitten by a snake, act quickly.

The definitive treatment for snake-venom poisoning is the proper administration of antivenom. Get the victim to a hospital immediately.

Keep the victim calm. Increased activity can spread the venom and the illness. Retreat out of snake's striking range, but try to identify it. If you cannot do this easily, kill the snake with a blow to the head, and take it to the medical facility so the authorities can identify it and estimate the amount of antivenom necessary. (Remember to carry the snake in a container so that the jaws' reflex action cannot harm someone else.) Check for signs of envenomation.

Immediately transport the victim to the nearest hospital. If possible, splint the body part that was bitten, to avoid unnecessary motion. If a limb was bitten, keep it at a level below the heart. *Do not apply ice directly to the wound.* If it will take longer than two hours to reach medical help, and the bite is on an arm or leg, place a 2"x 2", 1/4"- thick cloth pad over the bite and firmly wrap the limb (ideally, with an elastic wrap) directly over the bite and six inches on either side, taking care to check for adequate circulation to the fingers and toes. This wrap may slow the spread of venom.

First-Aid Kit

The following kit is suggested for those who have had no first-aid or other medical training. It costs about $15, weighs about a pound, and occupies about a 3" x 6" x 9" space.

Eight 4" x 4" gauze pads
Four 3" x 4" gauze pads
Five 2" bandages
Ten 1" bandages
Six alcohol prep pads
Ten large butterfly closures
One triangular bandage (40")
Two 3" rolls of gauze
Twenty tablets of aspirin-free pain-killer
One 15' roll of 2" adhesive tape
One 3" Ace bandage
Twenty salt tablets
One 3" x 4" moleskin

Three safety pins
One small scissors
One tweezers
Personal medications as necessary

References

1. Red Cross first-aid manuals.
2. *Mountaineering Medicine*, by Fred T. Darvill, Jr., M.D., Wilderness Press, Berkeley, 1985.
3. *Mountaineering First Aid: A Guide to Accident Response and First Aid*, The Mountaineers, Seattle, 1985.
4. *Emergency Survival Handbook*, by the American Safety League, 1985. A pocket-sized book and survival kit with easy instructions.
5. *Medicine for the Outdoors: A Guide to Emergency Medical Procedures and First Aid*, by Paul S. Auerbach, M.D., Little Brown & Co., Boston, 1986.

Shelters and Campsites

The Appalachian Trail in New York and New Jersey has a number of shelters and campsites. In most cases they are less than a day's hike apart.

The following is a north-to-south list of the shelters and campsites along the Trail in New York and New Jersey. Additional information is provided in the Trail data for the respective sections of the Trail.

Trail Sec.	Miles from Conn.	Miles from Pa.	Shelter
N.Y. 2	1.1	162.5	Wiley (Webatuck) Shelter
N.Y. 3	9.4	154.2	Campsites in Edward R. Murrow Memorial Park (3.1 miles from Trail) (fee)
N.Y. 3	10.1	153.5	Telephone Pioneers Shelter
N.Y. 4	17.4	146.2	Morgan Stewart Memorial Shelter
N.Y. 5	22.9	140.7	Bailey Spring Campsites (0.4 mile on side trail)
N.Y. 6	26.2	137.4	RPH Cabin
N.Y. 6	33.1	130.5	Fahnestock State Park Campsites (1.0 mile NE of Trail)

N.Y. 7	36.8	126.8	Dennytown Road Group Campsites
N.Y. 9	49.1	114.5	Hemlock Springs Campsite
N.Y. 10	57.2	106.4	West Mountain Shelter (0.6 mile on side trail)
N.Y. 10	60.5	103.1	William Brien Memorial Shelter
N.Y. 11	65.7	97.9	Fingerboard Shelter
N.J. 1	94.1	69.5	Campsite in Wawayanda State Park
N.J. 3	119.4	44.2	High Point Shelter (0.1 mile on side trail)
N.J. 4	123.6	40.0	Rutherford Shelter (0.4 mile on side trail)
N.J. 4	126.6	37.0	Mashipacong Shelter
N.J. 4	132.3	31.3	Gren Anderson Shelter (0.3 mile on side trail)
N.J. 5	139.1	24.5	Brink Road Shelter (0.2 mile on side trail)
N.J. 6	159.0	4.6	Campsite No. 2 (no water)
N.J. 6	160.6	3.0	Campsite No.1 (0.5 mile on side trail; no water)

In addition, thru-hikers passing through the Delaware Water Gap National Recreation Area (parts of New Jersey Sections Five and Six) may camp along the Trail, provided they choose a site that is at least 0.5 mile from developed access roads or the boundaries of the national recreation area. Campsites must be no more than 100 feet from the Trail. Additional information is provided under "Shelters and Campsites" in New Jersey Sections Five and Six.

Shelters are generally three-sided, with open fronts. They may be fitted with bunks or have a wooden floor serving as a sleeping platform. Water, a privy, a fireplace, and, in some cases, a table and benches are usually nearby. Hikers should bring their own sleeping equipment, cooking utensils, and a stove.

Shelters along the Trail are provided primarily for the long-distance hiker who may have no other shelter. People planning overnight hikes should carry tents. This is good insurance, since the Trail is heavily used, and shelters are usually crowded during the summer. Organizations, such as Scouts, should keep their groups small (eight to ten people, including leaders), carry tents, and not monopolize the shelters. Although shelter use is on a first-come, first-served basis, please cooperate and consider the needs of others.

If a shelter has a register, please sign it.

Shelters are for overnight stays only, and, except for bad weather, injury, or other emergency, please do not stay more than one or two nights. Hunters, fishermen, and other non-Trail hikers should not use the shelters as bases of operation.

Use facilities with care and respect. Do not carve initials or write on shelter walls. Do not use an ax on any part of the shelter or use benches or tables as chopping blocks. The roofing material, especially if it is corrugated aluminum, is easily damaged; do not climb on it. Avoid putting excess weight or strain on wire bunks; the breaking of one wire endangers air mattresses and sleeping bags.

Be considerate of the rights of others, especially during meal times. Keep noise to a minimum between nine p.m. and seven a.m. for the sake of those attempting to sleep.

Preserve the surroundings and the ecological integrity of the site. Vandalism and carelessness mar the site's pristine nature and cause maintenance problems. Never cut live trees. Keep to trodden paths. Be conservative and careful with the environment.

Leave the shelter in good condition. Do not leave food in the shelter; this may cause damage by animals. Remove unburned trash from the fireplace, including aluminum foil, and pack out food and refuse.

Campfires

Because of the danger of forest fires, open ground fires are prohibited along the Trail in New York and New Jersey (except in fireplaces provided at designated campsites). Carry a portable camp stove, and use it as a substitute for an open fire.

No matter how many people use a fire, all share in responsibility for it. Be especially alert for sparks blowing from fires during high winds.

Use wood economically. Use dead or downed wood only, even if this requires searching some distance away. Many campsites have suffered visible deterioration from hikers cutting wood from trees near the site. The effective cooking fire is small. If you use wood stored in a shelter, replenish the supply.

Upon leaving the campsite, even temporarily, ensure that your fire—to the last spark—is out. Douse it with water, and overturn the ashes until all underlying coals have been thoroughly extinguished.

Transportation to the Trail

Both the northern and southern ends of nearly all sections of the A.T. in New York and New Jersey are easily accessible by highways. The only exceptions are New York Section Thirteen and New Jersey Section One, which end at the New York-New Jersey state boundary rather than at roads. In addition, many other roads intersect the Trail in the middle of sections.

Bus or rail transportation is available to many end points of Trail sections or to nearby communities. Information on available public transportation is included in the general information preceding the Trail description for each section.

If no other transportation is available, you may wish to hitchhike. In New York, hitchhiking is prohibited on the roadway, defined as the travel portion of the highway between the outside white lines. Outside the roadway, hitchhiking is permited, provided a dangerous situation is not created. In New Jersey, hitchhiking is legal only when the person soliciting the ride is completely off the highway, including the shoulder. Hitchhiking is prohibited along interstate highways in both states.

Group Hikes and Special Events

Special events, group hikes, or other group activities that could degrade the Appalachian Trail's natural or cultural resources or social values should be avoided. Examples of such activities include publicized spectator events, commercial or competitive activities, or programs involving large groups

The policy of the Appalachian Trail Conference is that groups planning to spend one or more nights on the Trail should not exceed ten people, unless the local maintaining organization has made special arrangements to both accommodate the group and protect the Trail values.

The Hiker's Responsibilities

While most of the Trail in New York and New Jersey is on state or federal lands, some of it is still on private property. In all cases, the land the Trail crosses must be respected and treated with care. Only careful use will preserve the natural beauty of the Trail environment and ensure the integrity of the Appalachian Trail. Improper use can endanger the continuity of the Trail. Private landowners can promptly order hikers off their property and close the Trail route. Vandalism, camping and fires where they are prohibited, and other abusive use may result in Trail closure. Hikers should respect their natural surroundings and the property rights of people owning land along the Trail.

Do not cut, deface, or destroy trees, flowers, mushrooms, or any other natural or man-made features.

Do not damage fences or leave gates open.

Do not litter the Trail or campsites. Carry out all trash; do not bury it for animals to discover.

Respect the privacy of those who live near the Trail. Approach homes along the Trail only during emergencies.

Do not carry firearms; they are of no use along the Trail.

Be careful with fire. Extinguish all burning material.

In short, take nothing but pictures, leave nothing but footprints. Keep the wilderness, however near it be to "civilization," a place of quiet and spiritual renewal.

Conn. 341 (Kent) to Hoyt Road
Connecticut Section Six
11.3 Miles

Brief Description of Section

This section traverses the ridge of the Schaghticoke and Algo mountains, which allows many views of the valley below. It includes a section that follows the gorge of the Housatonic River below Bulls Bridge (one of two remaining covered bridges in Connecticut) and crosses the Ten Mile River on a 120-foot bridge. This is a very scenic area, although the section has two-and-one-half miles of road walking. Part of this section passes through New York, where the New York-New Jersey Trail Conference maintains the Trail. This portion is also known as New York Section One.

The portion between Bulls Bridge and Schaghticoke Mountain, which at present is mainly on roads, will be relocated to a protected corridor being acquired by the National Park Service. Be alert to the painted blazes, and, if they deviate from the printed Trail description, follow the blazes in preference to the printed data.

Road Approaches

Both the northern and southern ends of this section are accessible by vehicle. At the northern end of the section, the Trail crosses Conn. 341, 0.2 mile west of its intersection with Schaghticoke Road. Parking is available at the intersection, but overnight parking is not recommended. At the southern end, the Trail crosses Hoyt Road at the New York-Connecticut line, 0.3 mile south of its intersection with N.Y. 55. Parking for one or two cars is available near the Trail crossing. Road access is also available at Bulls Bridge Road. A parking area is just west of Bulls Bridge, 3.9 miles from the southern end of the section.

Public Transportation

At the northern end of the section, bus service to New York City and to Massachusetts via Bonanza Lines, (800) 556-3815, is available in Kent, Connecticut, 0.8 mile east of the Trail crossing on Conn. 341. At the southern end, rail service to New York City (Grand Central Terminal) via the Metro-North Commuter Railroad, (212) 532-4900, is available at the Harlem Valley-Wingdale station, 3.9 miles west of the Trail crossing of Hoyt Road.

Maps

For route navigation, refer to Map One with this guide.

For area detail, refer to the following USGS 7 1/2-minute topographic quadrangles: Kent, Connecticut; Dover Plains, New York-Connecticut.

Shelters and Campsites

Camping is permitted in two designated areas: Camping Zone 14, which includes the Mt. Algo Lean-to, located 0.3 mile from the northern end of the section, and Camping Zone 15, located near the bridge over the Ten Mile River, 3.0 miles from the southern end of the section. Water is available at both of these camping areas.

Supplies and Services

At the northern end of the section, meals, groceries, and a post office (ZIP Code 06757) are available in Kent, Connecticut, 0.8 mile east of the Trail crossing of Conn. 341. At the southern end, meals and a post office (ZIP Code 12594) are available in Wingdale, 3.3 miles west of the Trail crossing of Hoyt Road. (Follow Hoyt Road north for 0.3 mile, continue west on N.Y. 55 for another 2.5 miles, turn right and continue 0.5 mile to Wingdale.) Light meals may also be available on N.Y. 55, both 1.7 and 2.2 miles west of the Trail crossing of Hoyt Road.

Public Accommodations

Lodging is available in Kent, Connecticut, 0.8 mile east of the northern end of the section. A motel is on N.Y. 55, 4.5 miles west of the southern end of the section.

Trail Description, North to South

Miles	Data
0.0	From Conn. 341, ascend into woods.
0.1	Turn right on woods road for 75 feet, then turn left and reenter woods, ascending gradually.
0.3	Blue-blazed side trail to right leads 200 feet to **Camping Zone 14** , with **Mt. Algo Lean-to** and water.
0.9	Reach height of land on Mt. Algo, and begin descent.
1.2	Cross Thayer Brook and begin to ascend.
1.6	Reach crest of ridge on Schaghticoke Mountain and begin steady descent.
2.0	Reach large rock, with views to south, then continue to descend.
2.5	Reach viewpoint looking up the Housatonic Valley towards Kent. Trail continues along east side of Schaghticoke Mountain, with views of Housatonic Valley and U.S. 7 below.
2.8	Descend into Rattlesnake Den, a ravine with large hemlocks and jumbled boulders. Cross brook, a reliable source of water, and ascend gradually.
3.0	Reach open ledge, with good views.
3.1	Descend into Dry Gulch, another rocky ravine, then ascend steeply out of Dry Gulch and continue along east slope of Schaghticoke Mountain.
3.4	After ascent, reach Indian Rocks, a fine outlook to the east, on property of Schaghticoke Indian Reservation.
3.5	Trail comes out on open ledges, with impressive views to south and east. Soon reach rock with sign noting the crossing of Connecticut-New York state line. (Actual boundary is 700 feet ahead on Trail). This is the first of three crossings of the Connecticut-New York state line.

3.7	Reach height of land, and begin to descend gradually.
4.4	Turn left onto woods road, and cross brook.
4.5	Turn right as another woods road comes in from left.
4.7	Another woods road joins from left.
4.8	Turn left onto gravel South East Mountain Road.
5.0	Road begins to descend.
5.7	Pavement begins.
6.2	At Dogtail Corners, turn left onto paved Dogtail Road.
6.8	Pass granite state-line marker on left, and reenter Connecticut. Road changes name to Bulls Bridge Road.
7.4	Reach parking area, just before road crosses bridge over Housatonic River, and turn right onto old woods road.
7.7	Bear left, leaving road, and follow trail along west bank of Housatonic River.
8.2	Pass through gap in stone wall, and cross under powerline, with view of Ten Mile Hill ahead, then cross small brook.
8.3	Cross Ten Mile River on Ned Anderson Memorial Bridge, named in memory of man who laid out original route of A.T. in Connecticut and maintained it for 20 years. **Camping Zone 15** is in field near bridge. Turn right, and continue along south bank of Ten Mile River.
8.7	Turn left, and begin ascent.
8.8	Cross dirt road, with private property to right.
9.0	Turn right onto woods road, pass intermittent spring to right of Trail, and continue to ascend on footpath.
9.1	Turn left onto woods road.
9.3	Turn right, leaving woods road.
9.5	Reach top of Ten Mile Hill (1,000 feet), with limited views, and begin gradual descent.
10.3	Trail levels off.
10.6	Cross paved Conn. 55, and follow edge of field.
10.8	Cross brook, a reliable water source.
11.0	Cross end of field, and reenter woods.
11.3	Cross end of small field and reach Hoyt Road at the Connecticut-New York state line (end of section). To continue, turn right on road (see New York Section Two).

Trail Description, South to North

Miles   **Data**

0.0   From Hoyt Road, cross end of small field, and enter woods.
0.1   Reach top of ridge.
0.3   Cross end of field, and reenter woods.
0.5   Cross brook, a reliable water source, then follow along edge of field.
0.7   Cross paved Conn. 55.
1.0   Begin to ascend.
1.8   Reach top of Ten Mile Hill (1,000 feet), with limited views, and begin gradual descent.
2.0   Turn left onto woods road, and continue to descend.
2.2   Turn right, leaving woods road.
2.3   Pass intermittent spring to left of Trail, briefly follow woods road, then turn left, and continue to descend.
2.5   Cross dirt road, with private property to left.
2.6   Reach bank of Ten Mile River. Turn right, and continue along river.
3.0   Reach Ned Anderson Memorial Bridge. **Camping Zone 15** is in field south of bridge. Bridge is named in memory of the man who laid out original route of A.T. in Connecticut and maintained it for 20 years. Cross bridge, and continue along west bank of Housatonic River.
3.1   Cross small brook, then cross under powerline, with view of Ten Mile Hill looking back on Trail.
3.6   Continue straight ahead on dirt road.
3.9   Turn left onto paved Bulls Bridge Road.
4.5   Pass granite state-line marker on right, and reenter New York. Road changes name to Dogtail Road.
5.1   At Dogtail Corners, turn right onto paved South East Mountain Road.
5.3   At intersection with Aldrich Road, keep left.
5.6   Pavement ends. Continue straight ahead on gravel road, ascending gradually.
6.3   Road levels off.
6.5   Turn right onto woods road, and continue ascent.

6.6   Bear left at fork in road.

6.8   Bear left at another fork in road.

6.9   Cross brook, turn right, and continue to ascend.

7.8   Sign on rock notes crossing of New York-Connecticut state line. (Actual boundary is 700 feet back on Trail). Trail continues along east side of Schaghticoke Mountain, soon reaching ledges, with impressive views, to south and east, of Housatonic Valley and U.S. 7 below.

7.9   After ascent, reach Indian Rocks, a fine outlook to the east, on property of Schaghticoke Indian Reservation. Continue along east side of mountain.

8.2   Descend into Dry Gulch, a narrow, rocky ravine. Then ascend steeply out of Dry Gulch onto ridge.

8.3   Reach open ledge, with good views.

8.4   Descend into Rattlesnake Den, a ravine with large hemlocks and jumbled boulders. Cross brook, a reliable water source, then ascend steeply. Continue along east side of ridge, with views to east.

8.8   Reach viewpoint looking up Housatonic Valley toward Kent.

9.3   After ascent, reach large rock, with views to south, then continue ascent.

9.7   Reach height of land and begin descent off Schaghticoke Mountain.

10.1   Cross Thayer Brook, and ascend.

10.4   Reach height of land on Mt. Algo, and begin to descend.

11.0   Blue-blazed side trail to left leads 200 feet to **Camping Zone 14** with **Mt. Algo Lean-to** and water.

11.2   Turn right on woods road for 75 feet, then turn left and continue to descend.

11.3   Reach paved Conn. 341 (end of section). To continue, cross highway, and enter pasture on opposite side of highway. The description of A.T. continues in *Appalachian Trail Guide to Massachusetts-Connecticut*.

Hoyt Road to N.Y. 22 (Pawling)
New York Section Two
7.0 Miles

Brief Description of Section

This section is mostly woodland trails. The woods are second growth, ranging from scrubby to mature. Several fine groves of hemlocks are along the way, as well as good stands of mixed hardwoods along the Hammersly Ridge. Along the ridge, the Trail passes through several marshy areas. At a few points, one can catch glimpses of the rolling southern Dutchess County countryside. The elevation at Hoyt Road is 420 feet, and, at N.Y. 22, it is 450 feet. The highest point is on the Hammersly Ridge in the Pawling Nature Preserve, with an elevation of 1,053 feet.

This area was farmed extensively during Revolutionary times, but much of the land has reverted to forest, a large portion of which has been incorporated into large private estates, as well as the thousand-acre Pawling Nature Preserve owned by The Nature Conservancy. Evidence of the past can be seen in the crumbling stone walls, foundations, and dams and in the traces of abandoned orchards, fields and roads visible along the Trail.

Road Approaches

Both the northern and southern ends of this section are accessible by vehicle. At the northern end, the Trail crosses Hoyt Road at the New York-Connecticut line, 0.3 mile south of its intersection with N.Y. 55. Parking is available for one or two cars near the Trail crossing. At the southern end, the Trail crosses N.Y. 22, 1.1 miles north of Corbin Road and 2.4 miles north of the center of the village of Pawling. A designated parking area is north of the Trail crossing.

Road access is also available at Duell Hollow Road, which crosses the Trail 0.9 mile from the northern end of the section. Parking is available just south of the Trail crossing, near an old cemetery.

Public Transportation

Rail service to New York City (Grand Central Terminal) via the Metro-North Commuter Railroad, (212) 532-4900, is available at Pawling, 2.4 miles south of the Trail crossing of N.Y. 22 at the southern end of the section, and at the Harlem Valley-Wingdale station, 3.9 miles west of the Trail crossing of Hoyt Road at the northern end of the section.

Limited bus service to Pawling and Poughkeepsie, via Loops 2b and 4a of the Dutchess County Loop Bus System, (914) 485-4690, is available at the Trail crossing of N.Y. 22 at the southern end of the section.

Maps

For route navigation, refer to Map One with this guide. For area detail, refer to the following USGS 7 1/2-minute topographic quadrangles: Dover Plains, New York-Connecticut; Pawling, New York-Connecticut. Another reference is the map of Pawling Nature Preserve available from the Lower Hudson Chapter of The Nature Conservancy, Chestnut Ridge Road, Mt. Kisco, New York 10549.

Shelters and Campsites

This section has one shelter.

Wiley (Webatuck) Shelter. Built in 1940, with assistance from William O. Wiley of the Tramp and Trail Club of New York, on property of Camp Siwanoy, Westchester-Putnam Council, Boy Scouts of America; 1.1 miles from northern end of the section; accommodates 6; water available from cistern on Trail 0.1 mile north of the shelter.

Supplies and Services

At the northern end of the section, meals and a post office (ZIP Code 12594) are available in Wingdale, 3.3 miles west of the Trail crossing of Hoyt Road. (Follow Hoyt Road north for 0.3 mile, then continue west on N.Y. 55 for another 3.0 miles.) Light meals may also be available on N.Y. 55, both 1.7 and 2.2 miles west of the Trail crossing of Hoyt Road.

At the southern end of the section, a grocery store is located on N.Y. 22, 0.6 mile south of the Trail crossing. Groceries, meals, a post office (ZIP Code 12564), a laundromat, and other supplies and services are available in Pawling, 2.4 miles south of the Trail crossing of N.Y. 22. (Proceed south on N.Y. 22 for 1.2 miles, turn right onto Corbin Road for 0.4 mile, then turn left, and continue on Charles Colman Boulevard 0.8 mile to the center of Pawling.) The post office is on Broad Street, just west of the center of town. A supermarket (open seven days a week) is on East Main Street, 0.2 mile east of the intersection of Charles Colman Boulevard and East Main Street.

Public Accommodations

The southern end of the section has a motel 2.6 miles north of the Trail crossing. The motel can also be reached from the northern end of the section by following N.Y. 55, 4.5 miles to the west and south.

Trail Description, North to South

Miles	Data
0.0	From Connecticut-New York state line, proceed north on Hoyt Road.
0.1	Turn left and ascend through woods.
0.2	Follow posts across overgrown field, turn right onto woods road, then turn left and enter field. Bear right and follow along right edge of field.
0.3	Reenter woods.
0.6	Cross Duell Hollow Brook.
0.9	Reach paved Duell Hollow Road. Cross road diagonally to left, and reenter woods, soon beginning to ascend.
1.0	Pass cistern, a water source.
1.1	Pass through gap in stone wall, then turn left, pass in front of **Wiley (Webatuck) Shelter**, and recross stone wall.
1.2	Cross dirt logging road.

1.3	Trail levels off, then begins to descend.
1.5	Cross dirt Leather Hill Road diagonally to right, then begin to ascend.
1.6	Pass through gap in stone wall. In another 300 feet, cross stream.
1.8	Turn left onto old woods road.
2.0	Cross cleared strip of land (telephone cable). In another 90 feet, cross stone wall.
2.2	Cross stream.
2.3	Turn right onto grassy road that curves to left, passing Gate of Heaven Cemetery on right.
2.5	Turn right, and, in 65 feet, cross gravel road. Continue across overgrown field.
2.6	Turn right, and reenter woods.
2.9	Pass through gap in stone wall.
3.0	Pass through gap in stone wall and fence. In another 250 feet, cross stream on rocks.
3.2	Cross stream on logs.
3.5	Ascend steeply, and cross stone wall, then descend gradually.
3.6	Pass stone wall to left of Trail.
3.8	Enter Pawling Nature Preserve.
4.3	Cross swampy area on logs.
4.4	Turn right as red-blazed trail goes off to left. In another 125 feet, green-blazed trail goes off to right.
4.5	Cross swampy area on puncheons.
4.8	Cross stream. In another 200 feet, turn right as yellow-blazed trail continues straight ahead. Soon pass through mountain-laurel thicket.
5.1	Cross stream.
5.2	Pass swamp to right of Trail.
5.5	Begin to descend from top of ridge.
6.0	Continue to descend through field.
6.1	Reenter woods, soon crossing brook. In another 75 feet, please sign the register to right of Trail, which was installed by Pawling Nature Preserve.
6.5	Cross swampy area on rocks, and reach paved Old N.Y. 22. Turn left, and follow road.

6.8	Turn right, pass through gap in barbed-wire fence, and follow posts through field.
7.0	Reach N.Y. 22 (end of section). To continue, cross road and proceed south on N.Y. 22 (see New York Section Three).

Trail Description, South to North

Miles   **Data**

0.0	From east side of N.Y. 22, proceed east, following posts through field.
0.2	Turn left onto paved Old N.Y. 22.
0.5	Turn right, and reenter woods, entering Pawling Nature Preserve. Cross swampy area on rocks.
0.8	Please sign register to left of Trail, installed by Pawling Nature Preserve. In another 75 feet, cross brook, then pass through field, ascending gradually.
1.0	Bear left, and reenter woods, soon crossing old stone wall.
1.3	Turn right before reaching gap in stone wall.
1.5	Reach top of ridge, and begin to descend.
1.8	Pass swamp to left of Trail.
1.9	Cross stream.
2.0	Enter mountain-laurel thicket.
2.2	Turn left onto level trail as yellow-blazed trail comes in from right. In another 200 feet, cross stream.
2.3	Cross swampy area on puncheons.
2.6	Continue straight ahead as green-blazed trail begins on left. In another 125 feet, turn left as red-blazed trail goes off to right.
2.7	Cross swampy area on logs.
3.2	Leave Pawling Nature Preserve.
3.4	Pass stone wall to left of Trail.
3.5	Cross stone wall, and descend steeply, then ascend.
3.8	Bear left at fork. In another 125 feet, cross stream on logs.
4.0	Cross stream on rocks. In another 250 feet, pass through gap in fence and stone wall.

4.1	Pass through gap in stone wall.
4.4	Reach overgrown field, and turn left.
4.5	Cross gravel road. In another 65 feet, turn right onto grassy road.
4.7	With Gate of Heaven Cemetery to left, turn right, then immediately bear left on trail, and reenter woods.
4.8	Cross stream.
5.0	Cross stone wall. In another 90 feet, cross cleared strip of land (telephone cable).
5.1	Cross stone wall, and descend, soon following old woods road.
5.2	Turn right, and continue to descend on footpath.
5.3	Cross stream. In another 300 feet, pass through gap in stone wall.
5.5	Cross dirt Leather Hill Road diagonally to right, then begin to ascend.
5.7	Begin steady descent.
5.8	Cross dirt logging road.
5.9	Pass through gap in stone wall, then pass in front of **Wiley (Webatuck) Shelter**, turn right, and recross stone wall.
6.0	Pass cistern, a water source.
6.1	Reach paved Duell Hollow Road. Cross road diagonally to left and reenter woods.
6.4	Cross Duell Hollow Brook.
6.7	Emerge onto field. Follow along left edge of field, then turn left, immediately bear right, and descend on woods road.
6.8	Turn left and follow posts across overgrown field, then descend through woods.
6.9	Reach paved Hoyt Road. Turn right and follow road.
7.0	Reach New York-Connecticut state line (end of section). To continue, turn left and cross end of small field (see Connecticut Section Six).

N.Y. 22 (Pawling) to N.Y. 55 (Poughquag)
New York Section Three
7.0 Miles

Brief Description of Section

The northern part of this section climbs Corbin Hill, proceeds through open fields, and then steeply climbs West Mountain to a beautiful viewpoint over the countryside to the east. The southern part of the section has been relocated onto a protected Trail corridor acquired by the National Park Service, formerly the property of the United Nuclear Corporation.

The Trail does not pass close to the buildings that were once used by the United Nuclear Corporation for nuclear-fuel testing and research. The corporation ceased operating in December 1972 following an accident, when two nonnuclear explosions released plutonium dust into the surrounding environment. Following site decontamination, the Nuclear Regulatory Commission and the New York State Department of Environmental Protection cleared the site for "unrestricted use." Since that time, additional extensive testing has taken place, and elevated levels of radiation have been found in two of the buildings. The National Park Service is proceeding to clean the site completely and raze the remaining buildings. Please avoid the vicinity of the buildings completely. Until clean-up is completed, public access to the lake and buildings is prohibited.

The New York-New Jersey Trail Conference and the Dutchess County A.T. Local Management Committee endorse the use of the footpath through this property, because tests have not disclosed any unusual levels of radiation along the Trail route. (The Trail route comes no closer than a quarter mile to the lake and buildings.) It is a beautiful area, and we hope that you will enjoy walking through it. However, if you prefer not to walk through these woods, a roadwalk is maintained as a blue-blazed alternate trail. Please remember to stay to the side of the road and use caution when road-walking.

Road Approaches

Both the northern and southern ends of this section are accessible by vehicle. The northern end of the section is on N.Y. 22, 1.1 miles north of Corbin Road and 2.4 miles north of the center of the village of Pawling. A designated parking area is located just north of the Trail crossing. The southern end of the section is on N.Y. 55, about 1.4 miles southeast of its intersection with Pleasant Ridge Road and 1.5 miles southeast of its intersection with N.Y. 216. A designated parking area is located just west of the Trail crossing.

Road access is also available at County 20 (West Dover Road), which crosses the Trail 2.4 miles from the northern end of the section.

Public Transportation

Rail service to New York City (Grand Central Terminal) via the Metro-North Commuter Railroad, (212) 532-4900, is available at Pawling, 2.4 miles south of the Trail crossing of N.Y. 22 at the northern end of the section. Pawling may also be reached by proceeding south on County 20 (West Dover Road), which intersects the Trail 2.4 miles from the northern end of the section. Continue south on County 20 for 2.9 miles to the center of Pawling (after 2.1 miles, at intersection with Corbin Road and Lakeside Drive, the road name changes to Charles Colman Boulevard).

Limited bus service to Pawling and Poughkeepsie, via Loops 2b and 4a of the Dutchess County Loop Bus System, (914) 485-4690, is available both at the Trail crossing of N.Y. 22 at the northern end of the section and at the Trail crossing of N.Y. 55 at the southern end of the section.

Maps

For route navigation, refer to Map One with this guide. For area detail, refer to the following USGS 7 1/2-minute topographic quadrangles: Pawling, New York-Connecticut; Poughquag, New York.

Shelters and Campsites

This section has one shelter.

Telephone Pioneers Shelter. Built in 1988, with assistance from the White Plains Council of the Telephone Pioneers of America; 3.1 miles from the northern end of the section; 0.1 mile from A.T. on side trail; accommodates 6; water from stream crossed by side trail to shelter; privy 200 feet from shelter on side trail.

One public campground is also near the Trail.

Edward R. Murrow Memorial Park. Operated by Pawling Recreation Department, (914) 855-1131; at junction of Lakeside Drive and Old N.Y. 55, 3.1 miles from the Trail crossing of County 20 (West Dover Road), which is 2.4 miles from the northern end of the section (follow County 20 south for 2.1 miles, then turn right onto Lakeside Drive for 1.0 mile); open year round; nominal fee charged; swimming, hot showers, and snack bar available during season (Memorial Day to Labor Day); picnic shelters with fireplaces also available.

Supplies and Services

The northern end of the section has a grocery store on N.Y. 22, 0.6 mile south of the Trail crossing. Groceries, meals, a post office (ZIP Code 12564), a laundromat, and other supplies and services are available in Pawling, 2.4 miles south of the Trail crossing of N.Y. 22. (Proceed south on N.Y. 22 for 1.2 miles, turn right onto Corbin Road for 0.4 mile, then turn left, and continue on Charles Colman Boulevard 0.8 mile to the center of Pawling.) The post office is on Broad Street, just west of the center of town. A supermarket (open seven days a week) is on East Main Street, 0.2 mile east of the intersection of Charles Colman Boulevard and East Main Street. Pawling also may be reached by proceeding south on County 20 (West Dover Road), which intersects the Trail 2.4 miles from the northern end of the section. Continue south on County 20 for 2.9 miles to the center of Pawling (after 2.1 miles, at intersection with Corbin Road and Lakeside Drive, the road name changes to Charles Colman Boulevard).

The southern end of the section has a large grocery store (open seven days a week) at the intersection of N.Y. 55 and N.Y. 216, 1.5 miles northwest of the Trail crossing of N.Y. 55. A limited supply of groceries and light meals are available just west of the intersection of N.Y. 216 and County 7, 2.0 miles from the end of the section (proceed west on N.Y. 55 for 1.5 miles, turn left onto N.Y. 216 for 0.4 mile, then turn right onto County 7). Meals and a post office (ZIP Code 12570) are available in Poughquag, on N.Y. 55, 3.1 miles west of the end of the section.

Public Accommodations

A motel is located on N.Y. 22, 2.6 miles north of the northern end of the section.   A motel is also located on N.Y. 55, 2.6 miles west of the southern end of the section.

Trail Description, North to South

Miles	Data
0.0	From the end of New York Section Two, proceed south on N.Y. 22.
0.1	Turn right, cross railroad tracks, and continue through marshy area.
0.4	Cross stream on wooden bridge, then turn right, and begin steady ascent of Corbin Hill.
0.9	Pass through gap in stone wall.
1.1	Pass through large gap in another stone wall.
1.5	Reach top of hill. Trail levels off.
1.6	Emerge onto open field. Turn left, and continue along left side of field.
1.7	Cross barbed-wire fence on stile, then turn left, and follow posts across field.
1.9	Pass through gap in stone wall. In another 200 feet, cross marshy area on rocks, then pass pond to right of Trail, cross brook on wooden bridge, and cross barbed-wire fence on stile.
2.1	Cross stone wall on stile.
2.2	Cross barbed-wire fence on stile. In 300 feet, cross stone wall on stile.
2.4	Descend stone steps, pass huge white oak tree to right of Trail, and cross paved County 20 (West Dover Road).

	On opposite side of road, turn right, and follow posts.
2.5	Turn left, and descend slightly to cross wet area. Continue to follow posts through open fields.
2.6	Pass through gap in stone wall, and ascend over rocks, then pass old farm machinery.
2.7	Cross stream, and turn right, beginning steep ascent of West Mountain and paralleling stream on right.
2.8	Trail levels off, turns away from stream, and soon resumes steep ascent.
3.1	Side trail on left leads 0.1 mile to **Telephone Pioneers Shelter** (water usually available from stream crossed by side trail to shelter).
3.2	Trail begins to level off.
3.3	Side trail to right leads 100 feet to rocky ledge with beautiful views over farmlands below to east.
3.4	Reach summit of West Mountain, with good views to north, and begin gradual descent.
3.8	Pass swamp to right of Trail.
3.9	Cross dirt Penny Road (not passable by car). (Former A.T. route, now blue-blazed alternate trail, turns right onto Penny Road.)
4.1	After descent, cross brook, then cross swampy area on puncheons.
4.3	Cross stone wall, descend briefly, then ascend gradually.
4.5	Pass through gap in stone wall, and descend steeply.
4.8	Briefly follow old road that bisects rocky valley.
5.2	Pass swampy area to left of Trail, then ascend steeply.
6.1	Cross dry area between two swamps.
6.6	Go through narrow passage between rocks, and pass jumbled boulders to right.
6.7	Blue-blazed side trail to right leads to parking area on N.Y. 55.
6.9	Pass under powerlines.
7.0	Reach paved N.Y. 55 (end of section). To continue, cross road, and reenter woods (see New York Section Four).

Trail Description, South to North

Miles   **Data**

0.0   From N.Y. 55, proceed north on Trail, soon passing under powerlines.

0.3   Blue-blazed side trail to left leads to parking area on N.Y. 55.

0.4   Pass jumbled boulders to left, then go through narrow passage between rocks.

0.9   Cross dry area between two swamps.

1.8   After steep descent, pass swampy area to right of Trail.

2.2   Briefly follow old road that bisects rocky valley.

2.5   After steep ascent, pass through gap in stone wall, then descend gradually.

2.7   After brief ascent, cross stone wall.

2.9   Cross swampy area on puncheons, then cross brook, and begin to ascend.

3.1   Cross dirt Penny Road (not passable by car). (Blue-blazed alternate trail comes in from left.)

3.2   Pass swamp to left of Trail.

3.6   Reach summit of West Mountain, with good views to north, and begin to descend.

3.7   Side trail to left leads 100 feet to rocky ledge with beautiful views over farmlands below to east.

3.8   Begin steep descent.

3.9   Side trail on right leads 0.1 mile to **Telephone Pioneers Shelter** (water usually available from stream crossed by side trail to shelter).

4.2   Trail levels off briefly, then resumes steep descent, paralleling stream to left.

4.3   Turn left, and cross stream. Trail levels off.

4.4   After passing old farm machinery, climb over rocks, then descend, pass through gap in stone wall, and follow posts through open fields.

4.5   Descend slightly to cross wet area, then turn right, and continue following posts.

4.6	Cross paved County Route 20 (West Dover Road). On opposite side of road, pass huge white oak tree to left of Trail, ascend stone steps, and follow posts across grassy field.
4.8	Cross stone wall on stile. In 300 feet, cross barbed-wire fence on stile.
4.9	Cross another stone wall on stile.
5.0	Cross barbed-wire fence on stile, then cross brook on wooden bridge. In another 100 feet, pass pond to left of Trail, then cross marshy area on rocks.
5.1	Pass through gap in stone wall.
5.3	Near end of field turn left, then turn right, and cross barbed-wire fence on stile. Continue along right side of field, with woods to right.
5.5	Turn right, and reenter woods, soon beginning to descend.
5.9	Pass through large gap in stone wall.
6.1	Pass through gap in another stone wall.
6.6	After making sharp left turn, cross stream on wooden bridge. Continue through marshy area.
6.9	Cross railroad tracks, and reach N.Y. 22. Turn left, and continue along road.
7.0	Turn right, and cross road (end of section). To continue, follow posts through field (see New York Section Two).

N.Y. 55 (Poughquag) to N.Y. 52 (Stormville)
New York Section Four
7.1 Miles

Brief Description of Section

This section goes over Depot Hill, with several beautiful views from rock ledges. Except for a few short stretches along roads, the Trail is on footpaths through woods. The elevation at the northern end of the section is about 470 feet, and at the southern end it is about 850 feet. The highest point in the section is at the summit of Mt. Egbert on Depot Hill, which is 1,329 feet.

Road Approaches

Both the northern and southern ends of this section are accessible by vehicle. The northern end is on N.Y. 55, about 1.4 miles southeast of its intersection with Pleasant Ridge Road and 1.5 miles southeast of its intersection with N.Y. 216. A designated parking area is located just west of the Trail crossing. The southern end is on N.Y. 52, 0.3 mile north of the intersection of N.Y. 52 with Leetown Road and 2.2 miles south of Stormville (on Old N.Y. 52). No parking is available at the Trail crossing. Road access is also available at Grape Hollow Road and Mountain Top Road at the I-84 overpass, 1.3 miles from the southern end of the section, and at Depot Hill Road, which the Trail crosses 2.1 miles from the northern end of the section. Parking is available at or near these locations.

Public Transportation

Limited bus service to Pawling and Poughkeepsie, via Loops 2b and 4a of the Dutchess County Loop Bus System, (914) 485-4690, is available at the Trail crossing of N.Y. 55 at the northern end of the section.

Maps

For route navigation, refer to Map One with this guide. For area detail, refer to the following USGS 7 1/2-minute topographic quadrangle: Poughquag, New York.

Shelters and Campsites

This section has one shelter.

Morgan Stewart Memorial Shelter. Built in 1984 of prefabricated wood; 3.7 miles from southern end of section; 3.4 miles from northern end of section; 75 feet from A.T. on side trail; accommodates 6; water from well on 400-foot side trail leading downhill from front of shelter; privy located 200 feet from shelter on side trail.

Supplies and Services

The northern end of the section has a large grocery store (open seven days a week) at the intersection of N.Y. 55 and N.Y. 216, 1.5 miles northwest of the Trail crossing of N.Y. 55. A limited selection of groceries and light meals are available just west of the intersection of N.Y. 216 and County 7, 2.0 miles from the end of the section. (Proceed west on N.Y. 55 for 1.5 miles, turn left onto N.Y. 216 for 0.4 mile, then turn right onto County 7.) Meals and a post office (ZIP Code 12570) are available in Poughquag, on N.Y. 55, 3.1 miles west of the end of the section.

At the southern end of the section, groceries and sandwiches are available at a store (open seven days a week) 0.4 mile south of the Trail crossing of N.Y. 52. (Follow N.Y. 52 south for 0.3 mile, then turn right onto Leetown Road, and continue 0.1 mile to the store.) Groceries and light meals are also available at a store (open seven days a week) 2.0 miles south of the Trail crossing on N.Y. 52. Stormville has a post office (ZIP Code 12582) and a meat market that carries a limited selection of groceries (closed Mondays), 2.2 miles north of the Trail crossing of N.Y. 52. (Proceed north on N.Y. 52 for 1.7 miles, then turn right onto Old N.Y. 52, and continue for 0.5 mile.) Another store with a limited supply of groceries (open seven days a week) and a public telephone is 0.2 mile farther north, at the intersection of Old N.Y. 52 and N.Y. 216.

Public Accommodations

A motel is located on N.Y. 55, 2.6 miles west of the northern end of the section.

Trail Description, North to South

Miles	Data

Miles   **Data**

0.0   From N.Y. 55, proceed south on Trail.

0.2   Reach paved Old N.Y. 55. (Blue-blazed alternate trail comes in from right and rejoins Trail.) Cross road, descend wooden steps, and cross muddy area on rocks.

0.3   Cross wooden bridge over wide stream, then ascend railroad embankment. Cross railroad tracks, and descend from embankment. Cross small brook, and soon begin ascending.

0.5   Cross bed of intermittent stream, then turn right, and resume steady ascent.

0.8   Pass balanced rock to left as Trail levels off.

1.1   Resume steady ascent.

1.5   After brief descent, cross boundary of state forest (marked by yellow blazes on trees). In another 150 feet, turn right, cross stream, and soon resume gradual ascent.

1.7   Begin to descend.

1.8   Pass through narrow passage between rocks, then pass swamp to left of Trail. Continue descent.

2.0   Begin to ascend.

2.1   Cross unpaved Depot Hill Road.

2.7   Pass seasonal pond to left of Trail, then turn right, and descend through narrow ravine. In 150 feet from base of ravine, descend rock steps. Trail levels off.

3.0   Begin to ascend.

3.1   Reach rock ledge with good views to north, as Trail levels off.

3.2   Descend briefly over rocks.

3.4	Side trail on left leads 75 feet to **Morgan Stewart Memorial Shelter**. Trail from shelter leads downhill 400 feet to well, a dependable water source.
3.5	Pass U.S. Coast and Geodetic Survey marker on rock at summit of Mt. Egbert (1,329 feet).
3.7	Reach flat rock, and turn right. In another 200 feet, emerge on ledge with good views to west and south, then begin to descend from crest of ridge, steeply in places.
3.8	Pass old stone foundation to right as Trail levels off.
3.9	Descend steeply through mountain laurel, cross brook, and ascend.
4.2	Ascend steeply, pass through cleft in rock, then descend.
4.5	Descend into hollow, turn right, then left, and ascend.
5.4	Cross hollow, with swampy area to left.
5.7	Steeply climb road embankment, and emerge onto paved Grape Hollow Road. Continue straight ahead on Mountain Top Road, and cross I-84 overpass.
5.8	Turn right onto unpaved Stormville Mountain Road.
6.0	At dead end of road, turn left, and ascend on footpath into woods, then descend gradually.
6.3	Emerge onto overgrown field. Turn left, and follow path across field, with wide views of the Shawangunk and Catskill mountains to the north and northwest.
6.5	Cross stone wall, and reenter woods, then descend to cross small stream.
6.6	Pass through gap in old stone wall.
6.9	Continue to descend as footpath gradually widens to grassy woods road.
7.0	Reach paved N.Y. 52. Turn left, and continue along road for 0.1 mile.
7.1	Reach end of section. To continue, turn right, and reenter woods on footpath (see New York Section Five).

Trail Description, South to North

Miles	Data
0.0	Where northbound Trail reaches N.Y. 52, 0.3 mile north of Leetown Road, continue north along N.Y. 52.
0.1	Turn right onto grassy woods road blocked off by wooden posts, ascending gradually as road narrows to footpath.
0.5	Pass through gap in old stone wall, and descend to cross small stream.
0.6	After brief ascent, cross stone wall and emerge onto overgrown field, with wide views of the Shawangunk and Catskill mountains to the north and northwest.
0.8	Turn right, and reenter woods, ascending gradually.
1.1	After brief descent, emerge onto dead end of unpaved Stormville Mountain Road. Turn right, and follow road.
1.3	Turn left onto paved Mountain Top Road, and continue across I-84 overpass.
1.4	Reach Grape Hollow Road. Continue straight ahead, crossing guardrail, and steeply descend road embankment, reentering woods. Ascend gradually.
1.7	Cross hollow, with swampy area to right.
2.6	Descend into hollow, turn right, then left, and ascend.
2.9	Ascend through cleft in rock, then descend steeply.
3.2	Descend to cross brook, then ascend steeply through mountain laurel.
3.3	Pass old stone foundation to left of Trail. Soon begin ascent through mountain-laurel thicket, steeply in places.
3.4	Reach crest of Mt. Egbert, with good views to west and south. In another 200 feet, reach flat rock, and turn left.
3.6	Pass U.S. Coast and Geodetic Survey marker on rock at summit of Mt. Egbert (1,329 feet).
3.7	Side trail on right leads 75 feet to **Morgan Stewart Memorial Shelter**. Trail from shelter leads downhill 400 feet to well, a dependable water source.
3.9	Ascend briefly over rocks.

4.0	Reach rock ledge with good views to north, and begin gradual descent.
4.1	Trail levels off.
4.3	Ascend rock steps. In another 150 feet, climb through narrow ravine, then pass seasonal pond to right of Trail.
5.0	Cross unpaved Depot Hill Road. Begin to descend, then ascend.
5.3	Pass swamp to right of Trail. Pass through narrow passage between rocks, and ascend moderately.
5.4	Begin steady, gradual descent.
5.6	Cross stream, and turn left as Trail levels off. In another 150 feet, cross boundary of state forest (marked by yellow blazes on trees). Ascend briefly, then begin steady descent.
6.0	Trail levels off.
6.3	Pass balanced rock to right, and resume steady descent.
6.6	Turn left, and cross bed of intermittent stream.
6.8	Cross small brook. Climb wooden steps up railroad embankment, cross railroad tracks, and descend from embankment. Cross wooden bridge over wide stream.
6.9	Cross muddy area on rocks. Ascend wooden steps, and cross paved Old N.Y. 55. (Blue-blazed alternate trail turns left onto Old N.Y. 55.)
7.1	Reach paved N.Y. 55 (end of section). To continue, cross road, and reenter woods (see New York Section Three).

N.Y. 52 (Stormville) to Taconic State Parkway
New York Section Five
4.7 Miles

Brief Description of Section

This section of the Trail traverses the multiple summits of Stormville Mountain and the western side of Hosner Mountain (not reaching the ridge itself). Good views are to the north and west, over the Hudson River Valley. Elevation at N.Y. 52 is 800 feet; at the Taconic State Parkway, 540 feet. The section's highest elevation is about 1,040 feet, on Hosner Mountain.

Road Approaches

Both the northern and southern ends of this section are accessible by vehicle. The northern end is on N.Y. 52, 0.3 mile north of the intersection of N.Y. 52 with Leetown Road and 2.2 miles south of Stormville (on Old N.Y. 52). The southern end is at the intersection of the Taconic State Parkway with Miller Hill Road.

Public Transportation

Public transportation is not available to either end of this section.

Maps

For route navigation, refer to Map Two with this guide. For area detail, refer to the following USGS 7 1/2-minute topographic quadrangles: Poughquag, New York; Hopewell Junction, New York.

Shelters and Campsites

This section of the Trail has one campsite.
Bailey Spring Campsites. 1.8 miles from northern end of section, on

0.4-mile side trail; water available from spring; no other facilities are available.

Supplies and Services

A store (open seven days a week), at the northern end of the section, 0.4 mile south of the Trail crossing of N.Y. 52, has groceries and sandwiches. (Follow N.Y. 52 south for 0.3 mile, then turn right onto Leetown Road, and continue 0.1 mile to the store.) Groceries and light meals are also available at a store (open seven days a week) 2.0 miles south of the Trail crossing on N.Y. 52. Stormville has a post office (ZIP Code 12582) and a meat market that carries a limited supply of groceries (closed Mondays), 2.2 miles north of the Trail crossing of N.Y. 52. (Proceed north on N.Y. 52 for 1.7 miles, then turn right onto Old N.Y. 52, and continue for 0.5 mile.) A store with a limited selection of groceries (open seven days a week) and a public telephone is 0.2 mile farther north, at the intersection of Old N.Y. 52 and N.Y. 216.

At the southern end, groceries are available in Shenandoah, on Miller Hill Road, 1.2 miles north of the intersection of Miller Hill Road with the Taconic State Parkway.

Public Accommodations

No accommodations are available in this section.

Trail Description, North to South

Miles	Data
0.0	From N.Y. 52, climb rock steps, and ascend gradually through mountain-laurel thicket.
0.4	Reach first summit of Stormville Mountain, and begin descent.
0.7	Pass old trail to right, which led to private campground (now closed), and begin ascent of second summit of Stormville Mountain.
0.8	Reach top of ascent, and continue along shoulder of ridge. Trail levels off and soon begins to descend.

1.2	Begin steeper descent, soon passing through hemlocks.
1.3	Trail makes sharp left turn, levels off, then descends more moderately.
1.5	Cross small brook, and reach paved Hosner Mountain Road. Cross road, and begin to ascend.
1.8	Blue-blazed side trail to right leads 0.4 mile to **Bailey Spring**, a water source, with adjacent **campsites**. Continue along west slope of Hosner Mountain, paralleling ridge.
2.1	Pass through thick hemlock grove.
2.4	To right are views north and west over the Hudson River Valley, with intersection of I-84 and the Taconic State Parkway below. Trail continues along shoulder of ridge, with many short ascents and descents.
3.2	Pass through semicleared, logged area. This section may be wet at times. It has some high, dense brambles.
3.4	Cross small brook.
3.6	Trail joins grassy woods road and begins steady descent.
3.9	Pass rock ledges and boulder outcroppings to left of Trail. In another 200 feet, veer off to left at stone wall, leaving the woods road. Trail levels off.
4.3	Resume gradual descent.
4.5	Pass through hemlock grove.
4.6	Turn left on unpaved road that runs parallel to Taconic State Parkway.
4.7	Turn right onto Miller Hill Road, and reach Taconic State Parkway (end of section). To continue, cross parkway, and proceed west on Miller Hill Road (see New York Section Six).

Trail Description, South to North

Miles   **Data**

0.0	From Taconic State Parkway at Miller Hill Road, proceed east on Miller Hill Road for 50 feet, then turn left onto unpaved road that runs parallel to parkway.

0.1	Turn right, leaving road, and begin ascent of Hosner Mountain.
0.2	Pass through hemlock grove.
0.8	Veer to right at stone wall and join old woods road, continuing gradual ascent. In another 200 feet, pass rock ledges and boulder outcroppings to right of Trail.
1.1	Trail becomes a footpath, passing through a semicleared, logged area, with high, dense brambles.
1.3	Cross small brook. Continue along shoulder of ridge of Hosner Mountain, with many short ascents and descents.
2.5	To left are views north and west over the Hudson River Valley, with intersection of I-84 and the Taconic State Parkway directly below.
2.6	Pass through large hemlock grove.
2.9	Blue-blazed side trail to left leads 0.4 mile to **Bailey Spring,** a water source, with adjacent **campsites.** Begin to descend.
3.2	Reach paved Hosner Mountain Road. Cross road, then cross small brook, and begin gradual ascent of first summit of Stormville Mountain.
3.4	Make sharp right turn, and ascend steeply through hemlock grove.
3.8	Reach top of ascent, with limited views over the Hudson River Valley to left through trees. Soon begin descent.
4.0	At base of descent, pass old trail to left, which led to private campground (now closed), then begin ascent of second summit of Stormville Mountain.
4.3	Reach second summit of Stormville Mountain, and begin to descend through mountain laurel thicket.
4.7	Reach paved N.Y. 52 (end of section). To continue, turn left (north) on N.Y. 52 for 0.1 mile, then cross road, and reenter woods (see New York Section Four).

Taconic State Parkway to N.Y. 301
New York Section Six
7.3 Miles

Brief Description of Section

The Trail in this section passes over the summit of Shenandoah Mountain, with many good views on both sides of the Trail. The southern portion of the section passes through Clarence Fahnestock Memorial State Park, with a beautiful viewpoint over Canopus Lake. The elevation at the Taconic State Parkway is 540 feet, and, at N.Y. 301, it is 930 feet. The highest elevation on the section is 1,282 feet, at the summit of Shenandoah Mountain.

Road Approaches

Both the northern and southern ends of this section are accessible by vehicle. At the northern end, the Trail crosses the Taconic State Parkway at Miller Hill Road. No parking is available at the parkway crossing, but parking for six to eight cars is available at the Trail crossing of Hortontown Road, 0.4 mile from the northern end of the section. At the southern end of the section, the Trail crosses N.Y. 301 at the southern tip of Canopus Lake in Fahnestock State Park, 1.5 miles southwest of the junction of N.Y. 301 and the Taconic State Parkway. Ample parking is available 0.2 mile northeast of the Trail crossing on Route 301. The Trail is also accessible from Long Hill Road, which crosses the Trail 2.7 miles from the northern end of the section.

Public Transportation

Public transportation is not available to either end of this section.

Maps

For route navigation, refer to Map Two with this guide. For area detail, refer to the following USGS 7 1/2-minute topographic quadrangles: Hopewell Junction, New York; Oscawana Lake, New York. Another good reference is NY-NJ TC Trail Map No. 15 (Central Putnam County-Fahnestock State Park).

Shelters and Campsites

This section of the Trail has one shelter.

RPH Cabin. Established by Ralph's Peak Hikers, formerly a local hiking club; located at Trail crossing of Hortontown Road, 0.4 mile from the northern end of the section (275A Hortontown Road, Hopewell Junction, N.Y. 12533); accommodates 15; open May-September only (caretaker on duty in evenings); water available. This shelter may be used by thru-hikers as a mail drop; packages will be held by the caretaker if sent to the shelter address.

In addition, a campground is located near the southern end of the section.

Fahnestock State Park Campsites. Maintained by Fahnestock State Park; on the southern side of N.Y. 301, 1.0 mile northeast of the Trail crossing at the southern end of the section; hot showers, flush toilets, and rain shelters available; no fee for thru-hikers.

Supplies and Services

At the northern end of the section, groceries are available in Shenandoah, on Miller Hill Road, 1.2 miles north of the intersection of Miller Hill Road with the Taconic State Parkway.

In addition, a seasonal hot-dog and ice-cream stand is at the beach at the northern end of Canopus Lake. Cold showers and swimming are also available. From the viewpoint overlooking Canopus Lake (5.0 miles from the northern end of the section, 2.3 miles from the southern end), follow unmarked trail steeply down to lake shore, and proceed for about 0.2 mile along shore.

Public Accommodations

No accommodations are available in this section.

Trail Description, North to South

Miles	Data
0.0	From Taconic State Parkway at Miller Hill Road, proceed west on Miller Hill Road for 250 feet, then turn left, and enter woods.
0.1	Cross bridge over brook. Descend through hemlock grove between stone walls.
0.2	Turn right, and cross stone wall.
0.3	Descend rock steps, and cross Hortontown Road. **RPH Cabin** is on left side of Trail, 300 feet beyond road crossing. Continue through field.
0.4	Cross bridge over brook, then follow puncheons over swampy area. Begin to ascend, crossing several stone walls.
0.6	Cross stream, and begin steep ascent.
0.8	Trail levels off.
1.0	Pass through hemlock grove.
1.2	Cross stream, and continue ascent.
1.3	Reach summit, with views through trees to east, then begin to descend.
1.6	Begin steep ascent.
1.7	Turn right at viewpoint to east, and soon continue to ascend rather steeply.
1.9	Pass through gap in stone wall.
2.0	Trail levels off and soon begins to descend.
2.1	Cross clearing for powerlines.
2.4	Cross intermittent stream.
2.5	Begin to ascend.
2.7	Cross Long Hill Road, and continue steady ascent.
3.0	To right of Trail is viewpoint to west.
3.1	Reach open summit of Shenandoah Mountain (1,282 feet), with beautiful views to east and views through trees to west. Begin to descend.

3.5	Trail levels off and joins old woods road, with stone wall to left.
4.2	Cross intermittent stream, and continue along stone wall, soon passing ruins of old building.
4.3	Turn right, leaving road.
4.5	Cross small stream.
4.7	Begin to ascend rather steeply, then more moderately.
4.8	Trail levels off.
4.9	Side trail leads to viewpoint to west through trees. In another 275 feet, reach better viewpoint to west.
5.0	Reach beautiful viewpoint over Canopus Lake at north end of lake. Begin to descend, steeply in places.
5.3	Cross small stream. Continue to parallel west shore of lake, with views of the lake below through the trees.
6.4	Cross rocky stream, and continue along shoulder of ridge on western side of Canopus Lake.
6.9	Begin descent to N.Y. 301.
7.0	Trail register is on tree to left of Trail. Please sign.
7.1	After steep descent, turn left, and follow powerline parallel to road.
7.2	Ascend from ravine, then turn right, and reach N.Y. 301. Turn left, and follow road.
7.3	Reach southern end of Canopus Lake (end of section). To continue, cross road, and reenter woods (see New York Section Seven).

Trail Description, South to North

Miles   **Data**

0.0	From southern end of Canopus Lake, proceed west along N.Y. 301.
0.1	Turn right, and enter woods, then turn left, and follow powerline parallel to road.
0.2	Turn right, and ascend steeply, then more gradually.
0.3	Trail register is on tree to right of Trail. Please sign.
0.4	Trail levels off, then begins to descend.
0.9	Cross rocky stream, and continue to parallel west shore of lake, with some views of the lake through the trees.

2.0	Cross small stream.
2.2	Begin steep climb.
2.3	Reach beautiful viewpoint over Canopus Lake at northern end of lake.
2.4	Reach viewpoint to west. In another 275 feet, side trail leads to another viewpoint to west.
2.5	Begin to descend, first moderately and then more steeply.
2.8	Cross small stream.
3.0	Turn left, and join old woods road bordered by stone walls.
3.1	Pass ruins of old building. Cross intermittent stream, and continue along stone wall.
3.8	Leave woods road, and begin to ascend.
4.2	Reach open summit of Shenandoah Mountain (1,282 feet), with beautiful views to east and views through trees to west. Begin to descend.
4.3	Viewpoint to west is to left of Trail. Continue steady descent.
4.6	Cross Long Hill Road, and continue to descend.
4.8	Trail levels off.
4.9	Cross intermittent stream.
5.2	Cross clearing for powerlines.
5.3	Begin descent.
5.4	Pass through gap in stone wall, and continue to descend, steeply in places.
5.6	Turn left at viewpoint to east, and descend steeply.
6.0	After ascent, reach summit, with views through trees to east, then begin to descend.
6.1	Cross stream, and continue descent.
6.3	Pass through hemlock grove.
6.5	Begin steep descent.
6.7	Cross stream, then continue to descend more gradually, crossing several stone walls.
6.9	Follow puncheons over swampy area. Cross bridge over brook, and continue on grassy path through field. In another 400 feet, **RPH Cabin** is to right of Trail.
7.0	Cross Hortontown Road, and ascend rock steps.
7.1	Cross stone wall. Turn left, following path between two stone walls, and ascend. Soon pass through hemlocks.

7.2   Cross bridge over brook. In another 250 feet, turn right
        onto Miller Hill Road.
7.3   Reach Taconic State Parkway (end of section). To con-
        tinue, cross parkway, and turn left onto unpaved road
        (see New York Section Five).

N.Y. 301 to Canopus Hill Road
New York Section Seven
7.5 Miles

Brief Description of Section

Most of this section is in Clarence Fahnestock Memorial State Park. At the northern end, the Trail follows a narrow-gauge railroad bed built in 1862 to transport ore from Sunk Mine to Cold Spring Turnpike. Elevation at N.Y. 301 is 914 feet; at Canopus Hill Road, 420 feet. The highest point is 1,061 feet, on the ridge between Sunk Mine Road and Dennytown Road.

Road Approaches

Both the northern and southern ends of this section are accessible by vehicle. At the northern end, the Trail crosses N.Y. 301 at the southern tip of Canopus Lake in Fahnestock State Park, 1.5 miles southwest of the junction of N.Y. 301 and the Taconic State Parkway. Parking is available on N.Y. 301, 0.2 mile northeast of the Trail crossing.

The southern end is on Canopus Hill Road, 0.3 mile west of its intersection with Canopus Hollow Road at Canopus Valley Crossroads. Take U.S. 9 to Travis Corners Road. Proceed east on Travis Corners Road 0.8 mile to Old Albany Post Road. Turn right onto Old Albany Post Road, then left at the next intersection onto Canopus Hill Road. Continue east on Canopus Hill Road for 1.0 mile to the Trail crossing. Parking is not available here but is at Dennytown Road, which intersects the A.T. 3.7 miles from the northern end of the section and 3.8 miles from the southern end. To reach this point, follow Dennytown Road south from N.Y. 301 for about 1.2 miles.

Public Transportation

Public transportation is not available to either end of this section.

Maps

For route navigation, refer to Map Two with this guide. For area detail, refer to the following USGS 7 1/2-minute topographic quadrangle: Oscawana Lake, New York. Another reference is NY-NJ TC Trail Map No. 15 (Central Putnam County-Fahnestock State Park).

Shelters and Campsites

This section of the Trail has two campsites.

Fahnestock State Park Campsites. Maintained by Fahnestock State Park, on the southern side of N.Y. 301, 1.0 mile northeast of Trail crossing at northern end of section; hot showers, flush toilets, and rain shelters available; no fee for thru-hikers.

Dennytown Road Group Campsites. Maintained by Fahnestock State Park, on Dennytown Road at Trail crossing, 3.8 miles from southern end of section; water and latrines available; may be used only by thru-hikers; no fee.

Supplies and Services

Supplies and services are not available in this section.

Public Accommodations

Public accommodations are not available in this section.

Trail Description, North to South

Miles	Data
0.0	From N.Y. 301, enter hemlock grove, and follow bed of old mine railway, with Canopus Creek to left.
0.7	Trail turns left and leaves sunken railway bed.
0.9	Cross blue-blazed Three Lakes Trail. (To left, Three Lakes Trail leads back to N.Y. 301.)

1.1   Bear left, descend into small hollow, and ascend over knoll.

1.2   Enter level area that was once a farm. Turn right, away from swamp. In 50 yards, turn left, and ascend through hemlocks.

1.6   Reach top of ridge. Continue along ridge through hemlocks, with some good views on both sides.

1.9   Descend short, steep cliff. Ascend slightly, then level off.

2.1   Cross stream, outlet of swamp to right of Trail, on bridge.

2.2   Reach Sunk Mine Road. Turn right along road, then turn left into woods, and begin to ascend. Sunk Mine Road continues to junction with Three Lakes Trail, which can be used as an alternate route back to N.Y. 301.

2.8   Reach height of land, with view to west. Trail begins to descend, with views to south and east.

3.5   Cross outlet of swamp, formerly a beaver pond, on right. Turn right, and continue above the southern edge of the pond.

3.7   Emerge onto large open field. Continue along left side of field, and reach Dennytown Road. **Dennytown Road Group Campsites** and water (from pump) are available here. Cross road, and continue for 100 feet on joint route with blue-blazed Three Lakes Trail, then turn left as Three Lakes Trail continues straight ahead.

4.3   After ascent, steep in places, turn left onto horse trail.

4.5   Turn left, and reenter woods.

4.9   Cross red-blazed Catfish Loop Trail.

5.7   After steady descent, turn right onto woods road.

5.9   Turn sharp left, leaving woods road, and cross large boulder field. Begin to ascend, leaving Fahnestock State Park.

6.5   Cross bridge over stream, and turn right. In 150 feet, cross Highland Road, and ascend stone steps on opposite side of road.

7.5   Reach dirt Canopus Hill Road (end of section). To continue, cross road, and follow Trail into woods (see New York Section Eight).

Trail Description, South to North

Miles   **Data**

0.0   From Canopus Hill Road, proceed north on Trail.
1.0   Reach Highland Road. Cross road, and bear right, paralleling road for 150 feet, then turn left, and cross bridge over stream.
1.3   Reach height of land, and begin to descend.
1.5   Cross large boulder field, entering Fahnestock State Park.
1.6   Turn right onto woods road.
1.8   Just before reaching stream with broken-down bridge, turn sharp left, leaving woods road. Reenter woods, beginning steady ascent.
2.5   Cross red-blazed Catfish Loop Trail.
3.0   Turn right onto horse trail.
3.2   Turn right, leaving horse trail, reenter woods on footpath, and descend.
3.8   After briefly following joint route with blue-blazed Three Lakes Trail, which comes in from left, reach Dennytown Road. **Dennytown Road Group Campsites** and water (from pump) are available here. Cross road, and follow along right edge of large open field, then turn sharp right, and reenter woods.
4.0   After passing swamp, formerly a beaver pond to left of Trail, turn left. Follow east edge of swamp, then cross its outlet stream.
4.2   Ascend ridge, with views to south and east.
4.7   Reach high point of ridge, with view to west, and begin to descend.
5.3   Reach Sunk Mine Road. Turn right along road, then turn left into woods. To left, Sunk Mine Road leads to blue-blazed Three Lakes Trail.
5.5   Cross stream, outlet of swamp to left of Trail, on bridge.
5.6   Ascend face of short, steep cliff, then continue along ridge, through hemlocks, with some good views on both sides.

6.1   At base of descent, enter level area that was once a farm. Turn right towards swamp, then, in 50 yards, turn left, and ascend over knoll.

6.3   Ascend steeply, and bear right.

6.4   Cross blue-blazed Three Lakes Trail.

6.6   At trail register, A.T. turns right and follows bed of old mine railway, with Canopus Creek to the right.

7.5   Reach N.Y. 301 (end of section). To continue, turn left along N.Y. 301 (see New York Section Six).

Canopus Hill Road to U.S. 9
New York Section Eight
5.0 Miles

Brief Description of Section

The Trail in this section climbs over Canopus Hill and continues over Denning Hill and Little Fort Hill—a ridge of hills full of history. It crosses the Old Albany Post Road, which was the main land route from New York to Albany during the Revolutionary War.

This area saw considerable activity during the Revolutionary War. The Canopus Valley and Old Albany post roads were used by the Continentals to travel from Fishkill, a military supply depot, to Continental Village. The latter was the site of a troop encampment and still remains as a small village. On October 9, 1777, the British moved north from Peekskill and routed the 2,000 Continentals encamped there. The men took to the surrounding hills, most of which were fortified. The names on the land—Fort Hill, Little Fort Hill, Fort Defiance Hill, Gallows Hill—are reminders of that time. The Old West Point Road led to Benedict Arnold's headquarters at Garrison. It was also one of the roads taken by the military escort with Major Andre, then a captive, from headquarters in North Salem to Garrison, after the flight of the traitorous Arnold.

Elevation at Canopus Hill Road is 420 feet; at U.S. 9 it is 400 feet. The highest elevation is 900 feet, at the top of Denning Hill.

Road Approaches

Both the northern and southern ends of this section are accessible by vehicle. Parking is not available at the northern end, where the Trail crosses Canopus Hill Road 0.3 mile west of its intersection with Canopus Hollow Road at Canopus Valley Crossroads. At the southern end, the Trail crosses U.S. 9 at its intersection with N.Y. 403, 0.5 mile north of the Graymoor monastery and 4.0 miles north of the U.S. 9-U.S. 6/202 intersection just north of Peekskill. Parking is available on a short road between U.S. 9 and N.Y. 403, about 0.1 mile north of the Trail crossing.

Public Transportation

At the southern end of the section, bus service to New York City via Leprechaun Lines, (914) 896-4600, is available on U.S. 9 at the entrance to the Graymoor monastery, 0.5 mile south of the Trail crossing. No public transportation is available at the northern end of the section.

Maps

For route navigation, refer to Map Two with this guide. For area detail, refer to the following USGS 7 1/2-minute topographic quadrangles: West Point, New York; Peekskill, New York. Additional references are NY-NJ TC Trail Map No. 1 (Anthony's Nose-Canada Hill) and NY-NJ TC Trail Map No. 15 (Central Putnam County-Fahnestock State Park).

Shelters and Campsites

No shelters or campsites are available in this section.

Supplies and Services

At the southern end of the section, meals may be obtained at the Bavarian Inn, on U.S. 9, 0.8 mile south of the Trail crossing. Groceries and sandwiches are available at a store located at the intersection of U.S. 9 and South Mountain Pass, 1.9 miles south of the Trail crossing (open seven days a week). A variety of supplies and services is available in Peekskill, about 4.8 miles from the southern end of the section. From the Trail crossing of U.S. 9, proceed south on U.S. 9 for 3.1 miles, then follow Highland Avenue to the center of Peekskill.

Public Accommodations

Motels are available in Peekskill, 4.8 miles from the southern end of the section.

Trail Description, North to South

Miles   **Data**

0.0   From Canopus Hill Road, follow Trail to south, entering
        woods on footpath.
0.1   Cross brook, turn right, and begin moderate ascent of
        Canopus Hill.
0.4   Bear right, passing large hemlock to left of Trail, and
        continue to ascend more steeply.
0.7   Reach viewpoint in cleared area at top of Canopus Hill.
        Trail turns right and levels off. In another 300 feet, begin
        steep descent through mountain laurel.
0.9   Cross several stone walls as Trail ascends slightly.
1.4   Pass through gap in stone wall.
1.6   Pass through blueberry patch, and begin rather steep
        descent.
1.7   After crossing wet area on rocks, reach dirt Chapman
        Road at its intersection with Old Albany Post Road.
        Cross road, and reenter woods. In 125 feet, cross swampy
        area on puncheons, and ascend.
1.8   Bear left, and continue along side of hill.
2.1   Descend steeply over rocks.
2.3   Ascend steeply along rocky area, then continue to as-
        cend more gradually.
2.5   Cross stone wall, turn right, and ascend to viewpoint in
        clearing near top of Denning Hill, with good view to
        east. On a clear day, you can see New York City skyline.
        Continue along ridge for 150 feet, then turn left, and
        descend steeply.
2.8   Turn left onto woods road.
2.9   Turn left, leaving woods road, and reenter woods on
        footpath.
3.0   Short, unmarked trail to right leads to viewpoint. Trail
        descends steeply over rocks and follows ridge of Little
        Fort Hill.
3.9   Short side trail marked with orange tin-can blazes leads
        left to shrine of Graymoor monastery, with views to
        east.

4.3   After passing through overgrown field, reenter woods briefly, then emerge onto private gravel road. Turn right, and follow road uphill.

4.4   Cross paved Old West Point Road (paving ends at this point), and continue straight ahead along paved road. Follow road for 400 feet, passing farm building to right, then turn right, pass through grassy area, and enter woods, descending steeply for short distance.

4.5   Cross cleared strip of land, which curves to right, then continue along cleared strip.

4.6   Turn right, and reenter woods.

4.8   Cross dirt Old Highland Turnpike, then cross swampy area on puncheons.

5.0   Reach U.S. 9 (end of section). To continue, cross road, continue across gas-station property, cross N.Y. 403, cross stile over barbed-wire fence, and follow puncheons across pasture (see New York Section Nine).

Trail Description, South to North

Miles   **Data**

0.0   At intersection of U.S. 9 with N.Y. 403, proceed east, entering woods on footpath.

0.2   Cross swampy area on puncheons, then cross dirt Old Highland Turnpike. Continue on footpath through woods.

0.4   Turn left and follow cleared strip of land.

0.5   After brief, steep ascent, pass through grassy area, and turn left onto paved road.

0.6   Cross paved Old West Point Road (paving ends at this point), and continue downhill on private gravel road.

0.7   Turn left off gravel road, and reenter woods on footpath. Pass through overgrown field, and begin ascent of Little Fort Hill.

1.1   Short side trail marked with orange tin-can blazes leads right to shrine of Graymoor monastery, with views to east.

2.0	At top of rocky ascent, short, unmarked trail to left leads to viewpoint.
2.1	Turn right onto woods road.
2.2	Turn right, leaving woods road, and reenter woods on footpath.
2.5	After short, steep ascent, reach ridge of Denning Hill. Turn right, and continue along ridge for 150 feet to viewpoint in clearing, with good view to east. On a clear day, you can see New York City skyline. From clearing, continue briefly along stone wall, then turn left, and descend.
2.7	Descend steeply along rocky area.
2.9	Ascend steeply over rocks, then continue along side of hill.
3.3	After descending, cross swampy area on puncheons, and, in 125 feet, reach dirt Old Albany Post Road at its intersection with Chapman Road. Cross road diagonally to left, and reenter woods, crossing wet area on rocks, then ascend rather steeply.
3.4	Pass through blueberry patch as Trail levels off.
3.6	Pass through gap in stone wall.
4.0	Cross several stone walls.
4.2	Turn right, and ascend steeply through mountain laurel.
4.3	Reach top of Canopus Hill. Trail levels off. In another 300 feet, reach viewpoint in cleared area. Trail turns left and begins steep descent.
4.6	Pass large hemlock tree to right of Trail. Continue to descend more moderately.
4.9	Cross brook.
5.0	Reach dirt Canopus Hill Road (end of section). To continue, cross road, and follow Trail north into woods (see New York Section Seven).

U.S. 9 to Bear Mountain Bridge
New York Section Nine
5.8 Miles

Brief Description of Section

This section of the Trail passes through varied terrain. The northern end is a walk on trails and old carriage roads through woodland, with a magnificent viewpoint over the Hudson River. The southern part of the section includes a steep descent of the ridge of Anthony's Nose, with views across the river to the west. The Hudson Highlands can be seen at the crossing of the Bear Mountain Bridge. Elevation at U.S. 9 is 400 feet, and, at the Bear Mountain Bridge, 176 feet. The highest elevation is 840 feet on Canada Hill.

Many legends speculate on the naming of Anthony's Nose. Some early historians believed it was named in 1525 by Estevan Gomez, a Portuguese sailor, who referred to the river as "Rio St. Antonio." In fact, the village of Manitou, north of the bridge, was once called St. Anthonysville. Washington Irving's story in Diedrich Knickerbocker's *History of New York* claims it was named for Anthony Van Corlear, or Anthony the Trumpeter. Some believe that it was named for General "Mad" Anthony Wayne, who, among other exploits, led the successful march to capture the fort at Stony Point from the British in 1779. (A Bicentennial Trail in the Bear Mountain-Harriman State Park follows the march's route.) Two forts, Clinton and Montgomery, were built on either side of where the bridge now stands.

Road Approaches

At the northern end of the section, the Trail crosses U.S. 9 at its intersection with N.Y. 403, 0.5 mile north of the Graymoor monastery and 4.0 miles north of the intersection of U.S. 9 with U.S. 6 and 202, just north of Peekskill. Parking is available on a short road between U.S. 9 and N.Y. 403, about 0.1 mile north of the Trail crossing.

The southern end of the section ends at the tollgate at the western end of the Bear Mountain Bridge. No parking is available here, but parking is available along the shoulder of N.Y. 9D about 0.2 mile south of the point where the Trail leaves N.Y. 9D and ascends Anthony's Nose. Parking is also available at the Bear Mountain Inn, 0.8 mile south of the tollgate (fee charged in summer).

Note that this area has three Route 9s. U.S. 9, which crosses the Trail at the northern end of the section, is also known as the New York-Albany Post Road. N.Y. 9D, which is followed by the Trail at the southern end of the section, runs parallel to and near the Hudson River on the eastern side of the river and ends at the Bear Mountain Bridge. U.S. 9W is on the western side of the river.

Public Transportation

The northern end of the section has bus service to New York City via Leprechaun Lines, (914) 896-4600, on U.S. 9 at the entrance to the Graymoor monastery, 0.5 mile south of the Trail crossing.

At the southern end of the section, bus service to New York City via International Lines, (718) 389-8611, is available at the Bear Mountain Inn, 0.8 mile to the south on the Trail. Limited rail service (weekend only) to New York City (Grand Central Terminal) via the Metro-North Commuter Railroad, (212) 532-4900, is available at Manitou, 1.6 miles north of the point where the Trail leaves N.Y. 9D and ascends Anthony's Nose. (Walk north on N.Y. 9D for 1.0 mile, then turn left on Manitou Road, and follow for 0.6 mile to station.) Transportation to New York City is also provided by Dayliner excursion boats, operating in season from the dock at Bear Mountain.

Maps

For route navigation, refer to Maps Two and Three with this guide. For area detail, refer to the following USGS 7 1/2-minute topographic quadrangle: Peekskill, New York. Another reference is NY-NJ TC Trail Map No. 1 (Anthony's Nose-Canada Hill).

Shelters and Campsites

This section has one campsite.

Hemlock Springs Campsite. 3.5 miles from the northern end of the section; 2.3 miles from the southern end of the section; water available from spring.

Supplies and Services

At the northern end of the section, meals may be obtained at the Bavarian Inn, on U.S. 9, 0.8 mile south of the Trail crossing. Groceries and sandwiches are available at a store located at the intersection of U.S. 9 and South Mountain Pass, 1.9 miles south of the Trail crossing (open seven days a week). This store may also be reached from the Trail crossing of South Mountain Pass, 2.5 miles from the southern end of the section, by following South Mountain Pass east for 1.7 miles to U.S. 9.

At the southern end, meals are available at the Bear Mountain Inn, 0.8 mile south of the tollgate of the Bear Mountain Bridge. A post office (ZIP Code 10911) is near the inn. Fort Montgomery has meals, groceries, and a post office (ZIP Code 10922) 0.7 mile north of the Bear Mountain Bridge tollgate on U.S. 9W.

A variety of supplies and services is available in Peekskill, about four to five miles south of the Trail. From the Trail crossing of U.S. 9, walk south on U.S. 9 for 3.1 miles, then follow Highland Avenue to the center of Peekskill. From the eastern end of Bear Mountain Bridge, follow U.S. 6/202 to the center of town.

Public Accommodations

At the southern end of the section, accommodations are available at the Bear Mountain Inn, 0.8 mile to the south, and in Fort Montgomery, 0.7 mile to the north. Motels are available in Peekskill, 4.0 miles to the south.

Trail Description, North to South

Miles	Data

0.0   At intersection of U.S. 9 with N.Y. 403, cross stile over barbed-wire fence on west side of N.Y. 403, and follow puncheons across pasture. Cross second stile over barbed-wire fence, then bear left, and follow old woods road, with stone wall to left.

0.1   Turn right onto old carriage road.

0.4   At wood steps on left side of road, turn left, and ascend, steeply in places, on footpath into woods.

0.9   Turn left onto old carriage road (now merely a footpath), and continue along ridge of Canada Hill. (To right, carriage road leads to Sugarloaf, with good views.)

1.0   Blue-blazed side trail to right leads 100 feet to beautiful viewpoint over Hudson River, with Bear Mountain Bridge visible to left and West Point visible to right.

1.8   Unmarked side trail to right leads to Manitoga Nature Preserve.

2.2   Trail curves to right as unmarked trail goes off to left.

2.3   Please sign the Trail register on tree to right of Trail. Turn left, and leave old carriage road, continuing on footpath. (Straight ahead, old carriage road leads to Manitoga Nature Preserve.)

2.9   Begin steady descent.

3.3   Reach South Mountain Pass (a dirt road). Turn right, and follow road downhill for 250 feet, then turn left onto dirt road blocked off by large rocks. This road is property of National Guard at Camp Smith.

3.5   Turn right off dirt road. In 100 feet, blue-blazed trail to left leads to **Hemlock Springs Campsite** and spring, a water source. A.T. descends steeply on footpath.

3.6   Cross brook, pass through hemlock grove, and begin to ascend, first steeply, then moderately.

3.9   With stone embankment of road in sight ahead, curve to right, and continue to ascend on switchbacks.

4.1   Reach viewpoint to west over Hudson River. Continue

straight ahead through burned-over area, descending gradually. Avoid unmarked side trail to right.

4.3   Reach rocky dirt road (property of Camp Smith). Continue straight ahead on dirt road.

4.5   Turn right off dirt road, and descend steeply on footpath. Dirt road leads ahead to summit of Anthony's Nose, with magnificent views of Bear Mountain, Bear Mountain Bridge, and Iona Island to west.

4.9   With N.Y. 9D visible directly below, turn left, and follow relatively level path to south, parallel to road.

5.0   Reach paved N.Y. 9D at Westchester-Putnam county line. Turn left, and follow road.

5.3   Turn right, and cross Bear Mountain Bridge. Excellent views north and south along the Hudson River.

5.8   Reach tollgate at western end of bridge (end of section). To continue, turn left, and follow Trail through Trailside Museum and Zoo (see New York Section Ten).

Trail Description, South to North

Miles   **Data**

0.0   From tollgate on west side of Bear Mountain Bridge, proceed across bridge. Excellent views north and south along Hudson River.

0.5   At east end of bridge, turn left (north) on N.Y. 9D.

0.8   At Westchester-Putnam county line, turn right, and enter woods on footpath. Trail climbs, often steeply, up Anthony's Nose.

1.3   Reach dirt road (property of Camp Smith). Turn left, and follow road. To right, road leads to summit of Anthony's Nose, with magnificent views of Bear Mountain, Bear Mountain Bridge, and Iona Island to west.

1.5   As dirt road curves to right, continue straight ahead on footpath, soon passing through burned-over area. Trail ascends gradually.

1.7   Reach viewpoint to west over Hudson River. Continue straight ahead, and begin to descend. Avoid unmarked side trail to left.

1.9   With stone embankment of road in sight ahead, Trail curves to left and continues to descend, first moderately and then more steeply.

2.1   Make sharp right turn, soon continuing to descend, passing through hemlock grove.

2.2   Cross brook, and begin steep ascent.

2.3   Blue-blazed trail to right leads to **Hemlock Springs Campsites** and to spring, a water source. In another 100 feet, turn left on dirt road, property of National Guard at Camp Smith, and begin steady descent.

2.5   Reach South Mountain Pass (a dirt road). Turn right, and follow road uphill for 250 feet, then turn left, reenter woods on footpath, and begin steady ascent of Canada Hill.

2.9   Trail levels off.

3.5   Reach junction with old carriage road (now merely a footpath), with trail register on tree. Please sign. Turn right. (To left, carriage road leads to Manitoga Nature Preserve.)

3.6   Trail curves to left. Continue ahead as unmarked trail goes off to right.

4.0   Unmarked side trail to left leads to Manitoga Nature Preserve.

4.8   Blue-blazed side trail to left leads in 100 feet to beautiful viewpoint over Hudson River, with Bear Mountain Bridge visible to left and West Point visible to right.

4.9   Turn right into woods, leaving old carriage road, and descend, steeply in places. (Straight ahead, old carriage road leads to Sugarloaf, with good views).

5.4   Turn right onto old carriage road, and continue gradual descent.

5.7   At corner of fenced-in pasture, turn left onto old woods road.

5.8   Cross stile over barbed-wire fence. Follow puncheons across pasture, then cross second stile over barbed-wire fence, and reach N.Y. 403. Continue across gas station property, and reach U.S. 9 (end of section). To continue, cross road, and reenter woods on footpath (see New York Section Eight).

Bear Mountain Bridge to
Arden Valley Road (Tiorati Circle)
New York Section Ten
13.3 Miles

Brief Description of Section

This section passes through the northern portion of Harriman-Bear Mountain Park. From Bear Mountain Bridge at the northern end of the section, the Trail descends to an elevation of 124 feet in the Trailside Museum—the lowest elevation on the A.T. It then climbs to the summit of Bear Mountain (1,305 feet), marked by the Perkins Tower, and crosses West, Black, Letterrock, and Goshen mountains. Many beautiful views can be seen from the summits and ridges of these mountains.

The portion of the A.T. crossing Harriman State Park was the first section of the Trail to be completed. It officially opened on Sunday, October 7, 1923.

Financier and railroad magnate Edward R. Harriman (1848-1909) conceived the idea of establishing a park in this area. After his death, the park became a reality. In 1908, the State of New York acquired land around Bear Mountain to erect a prison. Due to the historical significance and scenic beauty of this land, the public objected to this proposal. Finally, in 1910, Harriman's widow, Mary A. Harriman, agreed to donate 10,000 acres of land to the state on the condition the state abandon its plan to establish a prison at Bear Mountain. Harriman-Bear Mountain Park expanded considerably in succeeding years, and many improvements were made under the supervision of Major William Welch, general manager and chief engineer of the park from 1910 to 1940. It was Major Welch who designed the diamond-shaped metal marker that became the standard symbol of the Appalachian Trail and who served as the first chairman of the Appalachian Trail Conference.

During very dry periods, trails in the park may be closed to the public to prevent forest fires. Hikers are advised to consult the staff members at the Park's headquarters at Bear Mountain or at the stone building at Tiorati Circle for alternatives.

For descriptions of the various trails crossing the A.T. in this section, as well as other trails in the immediate vicinity, consult the *New York Walk Book,* published by the New York-New Jersey Trail Conference and also available from ATC.

Road Approaches

Both the northern and southern ends of this section are accessible by vehicle. The northern end is at the tollgate at the west end of the Bear Mountain Bridge. No parking is available there, but ample parking is available at the Bear Mountain Inn, 0.8 mile to the south (fee charged in summer). At the southern end, the Trail crosses Arden Valley Road 0.3 mile west of its intersection with Seven Lakes Drive at the Tiorati Circle. No parking is available at the Trail crossing, but ample parking is available at the Tiorati Circle (fee charged in summer).

Public Transportation

At the northern end of the section, bus service to New York City via International Lines, (718) 389-8611, is available at the Bear Mountain Inn, 0.8 mile to the south on the Trail. Transportation to New York City is also provided by Dayliner excursion boats, operating in season from the dock at Bear Mountain. No public transportation is available at the southern end of the section.

Maps

For route navigation, refer to Map Three with this guide. For area detail, refer to the following USGS 7 1/2-minute topographic quadrangles: Peekskill, New York; Popolopen Lake, New York. Another reference is NY-NJ TC Trail Map No. 4 (Harriman Park-North Half).

Shelters and Campsites

This section has two shelters.

West Mountain Shelter. Stone structure; built 1928; 5.8 miles from the northern end of the section; 7.5 miles from the southern end of the section; 0.6 mile from the A.T. on blue-blazed Timp-Torne Trail; accommodates 8; water from spring 0.4 mile farther on Timp-Torne Trail.

William Brien Memorial Shelter. Stone structure; built 1934 by Civilian Conservation Corps; 4.2 miles from the southern end of the section; 9.1 miles from the northern end of the section; accommodates 8; water from spring-fed well on blue-blazed trail. This shelter is named in memory of the first president of the New York Ramblers, William Brien, who bequeathed funds to erect a shelter on the A.T. The original memorial shelter at Island Pond was removed and the name transferred to this shelter on Letterrock Mountain.

Supplies and Services

At the northern end of the section, meals are available at the Bear Mountain Inn, 0.8 mile to the south along the Trail. A post office (ZIP Code 10911) and the headquarters of Harriman-Bear Mountain Park are near the inn. Meals, groceries, and a post office (ZIP Code 10922) are available in the village of Fort Montgomery, 0.7 mile to the north along U.S. 9W.

At the southern end, refreshments may be obtained during the summer at the Tiorati Circle, 0.3 mile east of the Trail crossing of Arden Valley Road. A ranger station, bathing beach, and a public phone are located at the Tiorati Circle. Water is available from early May until November first from a faucet at the northeast corner of the circle.

Public Accommodations

At the northern end of the section, accommodations are available at the Bear Mountain Inn and in Fort Montgomery, 0.7 mile to the north along U.S. 9W.

Trail Description, North to South

Miles   **Data**

0.0   From tollgate at west end of Bear Mountain Bridge, turn left, pass through gate in fence, and enter Trailside Museum and Zoo. Reach Nature and Geology museums and Fort Clinton Historical Museum, then bear right, and follow paved path through zoo, past exhibits and memorials, including a statue of Walt Whitman. (If gate is closed—after 5 p.m.—continue straight ahead to traffic circle, bear left, cross U.S. 9W, and proceed to Hessian Lake straight ahead. Then turn left, and follow paved path along eastern shore of lake until A.T. is reached towards southern end of lake.)

0.3   Pass through gate, and leave Trailside Museum and Zoo. Immediately turn right, passing refreshment stand to right. Then turn right for 250 feet, turn left, and cross under U.S. 9W via underpass. Walk up steps, turn left, and follow paved path for 125 feet. Then turn left on another paved path.

0.6   Turn right towards lake. (Paved path straight ahead leads to Bear Mountain Inn.) After 100 feet, turn left, and continue on another paved path along eastern shore of Hessian Lake.

0.8   Reach playground area at southern end of lake. Turn left, cutting diagonally across playground, and reach junction of paved paths. Here Major Welch, Cornell, and Suffern-Bear Mountain (S-BM) trails begin. (Major Welch Trail provides an alternate route up Bear Mountain.) Turn right, and follow paved path (jointly with yellow-blazed S-BM Trail) uphill.

1.0   Cross under ski jump.

1.1   Bear right onto crushed-stone road. In another 150 feet, continue straight ahead as crushed-stone road curves to right.

1.2   Turn left, and cross stream.

1.4   Continue straight ahead as S-BM Trail leaves to left. In another 150 feet, pass under powerline.

1.8   Reach old paved road, the former route of Perkins Drive (now abandoned), and turn right. In 150 feet, reach dead-end turnaround of Scenic Drive, and continue straight ahead on road, with beautiful views to right of Hudson River, Bear Mountain Bridge, Bear Mountain Inn, and Iona Island.

2.1   Turn left and climb rock steps. Continue to ascend, with more views of the Hudson River and Iona Island.

2.3   Cross Scenic Drive.

2.4   Cross Scenic Drive again.

2.6   Pass plaque commemorating Joseph Bartha, pioneer trail builder, and reach summit of Bear Mountain (1,305 feet) at base of Perkins Tower, named for George W. Perkins, first president of the Palisades Interstate Park Commission. Beautiful views south to New York City skyline, west to Ramapo Hills, and east over Hudson Highlands. Turn left, and continue along edge of paved road.

2.7   Turn left, leaving paved road, and begin steady descent.

3.2   Reach paved Perkins Drive. Turn left, and follow road downhill.

3.7   Leave Perkins Drive, and turn right into woods.

4.2   Cross Seven Lakes Drive. Turn left on wide woods road, route of the 1777 Trail.

4.3   Turn right onto woods road, now a cross-country ski trail.

4.5   Fawn Trail, marked with bright red blazes, begins on right.

4.7   Turn right, leaving woods road, and begin steep ascent of West Mountain.

5.0   Reach beautiful viewpoint to east and southeast over Bear Mountain and Hudson River.

5.1   Blue-blazed Timp-Torne (T-T) Trail comes in from right and runs concurrently with A.T. In another 200 feet, reach second viewpoint over Bear Mountain and Hudson River, then turn right, and cross to west side of ridge.

5.2   Reach first of a series of viewpoints to west from rocky ledges on the west side of West Mountain. Swimming pool of Anthony Wayne Recreation Area is visible directly below. Continue along west ridge of West Mountain.

5.4   Climb to top of long, flat rock, then turn right, and descend. In another 375 feet, turn left, and again come out on rocky ledges, with good views to west.

5.8   A.T. continues straight ahead as T-T Trail diverges to left. **West Mountain Shelter** is 0.6 mile ahead on T-T Trail. A.T. soon begins to descend, steeply in places.

6.3   Turn left onto grassy Beechy Bottom Road.

6.4   Turn right, leaving Beechy Bottom Road, and descend into woods. In another 75 feet, cross stream.

6.3   Red-on-white-blazed Ramapo-Dunderberg (R-D) Trail comes in from left and runs concurrently with A.T. for next 3.3 miles. Trail register is on tree to the right of the Trail. Please sign. A.T. continues along woods road, now a cross-country ski trail (with red blazes).

6.7   Turn right, leaving woods road, and continue on footpath. In another 200 feet, cross Beechy Bottom Brook, a water source.

7.0   Reach Palisades Interstate Parkway. Cross parkway, and reenter woods.

7.1   Cross old woods road.

7.3   Cross 1779 Trail, descend briefly, then begin ascent of Black Mountain, steeply in places.

7.7   Trail comes out on open rocks on south side of Black Mountain, with beautiful views of Hudson River to east. On a clear day, New York City is visible to the south. Continue across ridge of Black Mountain.

8.0   Begin to descend.

8.1   Reach viewpoint to northwest over Silvermine Lake. Descend steeply over rocky ridge.

8.2   Cross fire road, now a cross-country ski trail, and begin ascent of Letterrock Mountain.

9.1   Descend steeply over rocks, and reach **William Brien Memorial Shelter**. Blue-blazed trail to left leads 250 feet to spring-fed well, a water source.

9.4   After ascent, reach rocky clearing, with views through trees to left.

9.9	At wooden bridge over wet area in saddle between Goshen and Letterrock mountains, A.T. turns right and proceeds over shoulder of Goshen Mountain as R-D Trail continues straight ahead to Tiorati Circle.
10.1	Leave old woods road, soon beginning to descend gradually.
10.3	Make sharp right turn.
11.0	Turn left onto fire road.
11.1	Cross Seven Lakes Drive diagonally to the left, and reenter woods.
11.3	Cross bridge over stream, and begin ascent.
11.4	Cross cleared area, and continue to ascend.
11.5	Make sharp left turn around switchback.
12.1	Reach rocky promontory with view to south over Lake Tiorati.
12.2	Turn left onto old woods road.
12.3	Turn left and reenter woods. In another 300 feet, turn left, and rejoin woods road.
12.5	Leave woods road, and continue on footpath.
12.6	Cross woods road. Soon begin steady ascent.
12.9	Descend over rocks.
13.3	Reach Arden Valley Road (end of section). To continue, cross paved road and reenter woods, following woods road (see New York Section Eleven).

Trail Description, South to North

Miles	Data
0.0	From crest of hill on Arden Valley Road, follow Trail north into woods.
0.4	Ascend over rocks. In another 250 feet, begin steady descent.
0.7	Cross woods road.
0.8	Join old woods road.
1.0	Turn right, and reenter woods. In another 300 feet, rejoin woods road coming in from left.
1.1	Turn right, leaving woods road.

1.2	Reach rocky promontory with view to south over Lake Tiorati; turn left into woods; soon begin steady descent.
1.8	Make sharp right turn around switchback.
1.9	Cross cleared area. Trail soon levels off.
2.1	Cross bridge over stream.
2.2	Cross Seven Lakes Drive diagonally to the left, and follow grassy fire road into woods.
2.3	Turn right, leaving fire road, and begin gradual ascent of shoulder of Goshen Mountain. (Fire road continues ahead to **William Brien Memorial Shelter**.)
3.0	Make sharp left turn.
3.2	Begin to descend on old woods road.
3.4	At wooden bridge in saddle between Goshen and Letterrock mountains, red-on-white-blazed Ramapo-Dunderberg (R-D) Trail comes in from right and joins A.T., with both trails running concurrently for the next 3.3 miles.
3.9	Reach rocky clearing, with views through trees to right, and begin to descend.
4.2	Cross old fire road, and reach **William Brien Memorial Shelter**. Blue-blazed trail to right leads 250 feet to spring-fed well, a water source. Immediately after passing shelter, Trail climbs steeply up rocky ridge.
5.1	Cross fire road, now used as a cross-country ski trail, and ascend steeply over rocky ridge.
5.2	Reach viewpoint to northwest over Silvermine Lake.
5.3	Reach crest of Black Mountain, with views to south. Continue along crest of ridge.
5.5	Trail comes out on open rocks on south side of Black Mountain, with beautiful views of Hudson River to east. On a clear day, New York City may be visible to the south. Continue across ridge of Black Mountain, then begin steep descent.
6.0	Cross 1779 Trail.
6.2	Cross old woods road.
6.3	Reach Palisades Interstate Parkway. Cross parkway, and reenter woods.
6.5	Cross Beechy Bottom Brook, a water source.
6.6	Turn left, and join woods road, now a cross-country ski trail (with red blazes), which comes in from right.

6.7   Trail register is on tree to the left of the Trail. Please sign. R-D Trail turns right at this point and leaves A.T. route.

6.8   Begin to ascend as Trail narrows to a footpath.

6.9   Cross stream. In another 75 feet, turn left onto grassy Beechy Bottom Road.

7.0   Turn right, leaving Beechy Bottom Road, and ascend steeply up West Mountain.

7.5   Reach open rock ledges on west ridge of West Mountain. Blue-blazed Timp-Torne (T-T) Trail comes in from right and runs concurrently with A.T. **West Mountain Shelter** is 0.6 mile to right on T-T Trail. A.T. continues along west ridge of West Mountain, with many beautiful views to west.

7.9   Turn right, and soon climb to top of long, flat rock, then descend.

8.1   Again come out on open ledges on west ridge of West Mountain, with swimming pool of Anthony Wayne Recreation Area visible directly below. After reaching second open ledge, turn right, and cross to east side of ridge.

8.2   Reach beautiful viewpoint to east and southeast over Bear Mountain and Hudson River, then begin to descend. In another 200 feet, A.T. bears right at fork as T-T Trail continues straight ahead.

8.3   Reach second viewpoint over Bear Mountain and Hudson River. Continue to descend rather steeply.

8.6   Join old woods road, now a cross-country ski trail, which comes in from right, and continue gradual descent.

8.8   Fawn Trail, marked with bright red blazes, begins on left.

9.0   Turn left on wide woods road, route of 1777 Trail.

9.1   Turn right, and cross Seven Lakes Drive. Reenter woods, and begin ascent of Bear Mountain.

9.6   Reach paved Perkins Drive. Turn left, and follow paved road uphill.

10.1   Turn right off Perkins Drive, and reenter woods, ascending steadily.

10.6	Reach summit of Bear Mountain (1,305 feet) at base of Perkins Tower, named for George W. Perkins, first president of the Palisades Interstate Park Commission. Beautiful views south to New York City skyline, west to Ramapo Hills, and east over Hudson Highlands. Turn right, and continue along edge of paved road.
10.7	Turn right, passing plaque commemorating Joseph Bartha, pioneer trail builder, and begin steady descent. In 150 feet, bear left on relocated Trail.
10.9	Cross paved Scenic Drive.
11.0	Cross Scenic Drive again and continue to descend, with views ahead of Hudson River and Iona Island.
11.2	Turn right onto Scenic Drive. Continue along road, with beautiful views to the left of Hudson River, Bear Mountain Bridge, Bear Mountain Inn, and Iona Island.
11.5	Reach dead-end turnaround of Scenic Drive, and continue straight ahead on abandoned road, the former route of Perkins Drive. In another 150 feet, turn left and descend steadily on footpath.
11.9	Pass under powerline. In another 150 feet, yellow-blazed Suffern-Bear Mountain (S-BM) Trail comes in from right and runs concurrently with A.T.
12.1	Cross stream, and turn right.
12.2	Join crushed-stone road coming in from left. In another 150 feet, join paved road coming in from right.
12.3	Cross under ski jump.
12.5	Reach intersection of paved paths at southern end of Hessian Lake. The S-BM Trail ends here, as do the Major Welch Trail (which provides an alternate route to the top of Bear Mountain) and the Cornell Trail. Paved path straight ahead leads to Bear Mountain Inn. Turn left and cut diagonally across playground area, then turn right, and follow paved path along shore of Hessian Lake.
12.7	Turn right, away from shore, on paved path for 100 feet, then turn left, and follow another paved path parallel to Hessian Lake. (After five p.m., continue along shore path to end of Hessian Lake, then turn right, cross U.S. 9W, follow it around traffic circle, turn right, and continue to tollgate of Bear Mountain Bridge.)
12.8	Turn right, then walk down steps, and cross under U.S.

9W via underpass. Turn right on opposite side of underpass for 250 feet, then turn left, passing refreshment stand to left.

13.0 Turn left, and enter Trailside Museum and Zoo. (If gate is closed, follow U.S. 9W to north, and turn right at traffic circle to reach tollgate of Bear Mountain Bridge.) Pass exhibits and memorials, including a statue of Walt Whitman, and proceed through zoo.

13.3 Pass Nature and Geology museums and Fort Clinton Historical Museum. Bear left, pass through gate in fence, and reach tollgate of Bear Mountain Bridge (end of section). To continue, turn right and cross bridge (see New York Section Nine).

Arden Valley Road (Tiorati Circle) to N.Y. 17 (Arden)
New York Section Eleven
7.5 Miles

Brief Description of Section

This section passes through Harriman State Park (see New York Section Ten for the park's history). The area in this section is filled with abandoned shafts, pits, and dumps of old iron mines, some of which date back as far as 1730. Tens of thousands of tons of magnetite ore were conveyed by oxen and horse teams over considerable distances to be smelted in the Greenwood Ironworks at Arden, which consisted of the Greenwood charcoal furnace built in 1811 by James Cunningham and the Clove anthracite furnace erected in 1854 by Robert and Peter Parrott. The pig iron was shipped by rail to Cornwall-on-Hudson, where it was ferried across the river to the West Point foundry at Cold Spring, to be made into the famous Parrott guns and shells, designed by the same brothers who operated the mines and furnaces. The Trail passes the Greenwood Mine along Surebridge Mine Road, which also leads to the Surebridge Mine and Pine Swamp Mine south of the Trail.

Between 1861 and 1865, Arden was a booming mining town, with a population of more than 2,000 engaged primarily in mining and smelting iron ore and producing charcoal used in smelting. Smelting with coal soon replaced smelting with charcoal, and the iron deposits of Pennsylvania and the Great Lakes region were much easier to mine (although not of as high a quality). By 1890, the mining industry in this area had all but disappeared.

In earlier times, this area was inhabited by many different tribes of Indians, most recently by the Algonquins. The hiker will find many Indian names. Ramapo means "formed of round ponds," used to denote a river in which potholes occur. Tuxedo is a word that may have been derived from P'tauk-seet-tough, which means "the place of bears," though it may have come instead from Duck Cedar, a name found on old maps of the area. Scattered through the park are lakes with Indian names, although these lakes are manmade and have no connection with the tribes that lived in the Hudson Highlands. Lake Tiorati, just east of this section of the Trail, means "sky-like." This lake formerly consisted of two bodies of water, Cedar Pond and Little Cedar Pond, which were first dammed unsuccessfully in 1767 by Baron Peter Hasenclever to provide a power source for his mines. One hundred-fifty years later, the ponds were again dammed, forming the present Lake Tiorati.

Elevation of the Trail at Arden Valley Road at the northern end of the section is 1,196 feet, and, at N.Y. 17, it is 500 feet. The highest point on this section is 1,328 feet, at the summit of Fingerboard Mountain.

During very dry periods, trails in the park may be closed to the public to prevent forest fires. Hikers are advised to consult staff members at the stone building just east of N.Y. 17 on Arden Valley Road or at the stone building at Tiorati Circle for alternatives.

For descriptions of the various trails crossing the A.T. in this section, as well as other trails in the vicinity, consult the *New York Walk Book*, published by the New York-New Jersey Trail Conference and also available from ATC.

Road Approaches

Both the northern and southern ends of this section are accessible by vehicle. At the northern end, the Trail crosses Arden Valley Road 0.3 mile west of its intersection with Seven Lakes Drive at the Tiorati Circle. No parking is available at the Trail crossing; however, ample parking is available at Tiorati Circle (fee charged in season). At the southern end, the Trail crosses N.Y. 17 at its junction with Arden Valley Road, 0.7 mile south of Arden. Parking for several cars is available on the east (northbound) side of N.Y. 17, 0.1 mile north of Arden Valley Road. Additional parking is available at the Elk Pen parking lot, 0.3 mile east of N.Y. 17 along Arden Valley Road.

Public Transportation

The southern end of this section can be reached from New York City and local points to the north by Short Line bus, (212) 736-4700. A flag stop will be made at the junction of N.Y. 17 and Arden Valley

Road. Scheduled stops are made at the Red Apple Rest in South-fields, 2.1 miles to the south on N.Y. 17. No public transportation is available at the northern end of this section.

Maps

For route navigation, refer to Map Three with this guide. For area detail, refer to the following USGS 7 1/2-minute topographic quad-rangles: Popolopen Lake, New York; Monroe, New York. Another reference is NY-NJ TC Trail Map No. 4 (Harriman Park-North Half).

Shelters and Campsites

This section has one shelter.

Fingerboard Shelter. Stone structure built in 1928; 1.1 mile from the northern end of the section; accommodates 8; water from Lake Tiorati (0.5 mile to the east on Hurst Trail) or from water faucet (summer only) at Tiorati Circle (1.4 miles to the north).

Supplies and Services

At the northern end of the section, refreshments may be obtained during the summer at the Tiorati Circle, 0.3 mile east of the Trail crossing of Arden Valley Road. A ranger station, bathing beach, and a public telephone are located at the Tiorati Circle. Water is available from early May until November first from a faucet at the northeast corner of the circle.

At the southern end, meals may be obtained at the Red Apple Rest in Southfields, 2.1 miles south of the Trail crossing on N.Y. 17. A deli, with a limited selection of groceries, is 1.8 miles south of the Trail crossing. The nearest post office is at Arden (ZIP Code 10910), 0.7 mile north of the Trail crossing. (Post office is in former Arden railroad station, 0.2 mile east of N.Y. 17 on secondary road.) A post office is at Southfields (ZIP Code 10975). A larger supply of groceries is in Tuxedo, 5.5 miles to the south on N.Y. 17. A public telephone is located at the Trail crossing of N.Y. 17.

Public Accommodations

At the southern end of this section, a motel is located in Southfields, 2.1 miles south of the Trail crossing on N.Y. 17.

Trail Description, North to South

Miles	Data
0.0	From crest of hill on Arden Valley Road, turn south onto woods road.
0.1	Pass round water tank to left, cross under telephone wires, and ascend into woods on footpath.
0.5	Reach summit of Fingerboard Mountain (1,328 feet), marked by stone fireplace to right of Trail. Descend gradually, then ascend slightly, following ridge of Fingerboard Mountain.
1.0	Blue-blazed Hurst Trail on left leads to **Fingerboard Shelter**, visible immediately below, and, in 0.5 mile, to Seven Lakes Drive at south end of Lake Tiorati. This trail was named for Harvey Hurst, a member of the Green Mountain Club, who opened the trail in 1922.
1.1	Trail turns sharp right and begins to descend, steeply in places, as red-on-white-blazed Ramapo-Dunderberg (R-D) Trail continues straight ahead.
1.6	At base of descent, turn left, and follow Surebridge Mine Road (also known as Lost Road) along Surebridge Brook, passing Greenwood Mine, now a water-filled pit, to left of Trail. During the Civil War, iron from this mine was hauled to the Greenwood Furnace in Arden.
1.7	Turn right, and cross Surebridge Brook. Begin ascent of Surebridge Mountain.
2.0	Reach height of land on Surebridge Mountain, and begin to descend.
2.3	After steep descent, turn left, and follow left bank of intermittent stream, then cross stream, and continue along right side of stream.
2.4	Turn right, leaving stream.
2.5	Cross blue-blazed Long Path.

2.6   Turn left, and begin ascent of Island Pond Mountain.
2.9   Reach summit of Island Pond Mountain (1,303 feet), and turn left as Arden-Surebridge (A-SB) Trail, with red-triangle-on-white blazes, comes in from right and joins A.T. Trail begins gradual descent.
3.2   Reach top of Lemon Squeezer, a narrow, steep passage between boulders. Descend very steeply. If descent is too steep, use bypass trail to the right. At bottom of Lemon Squeezer, A-SB Trail makes sharp left, while A.T. bears right. In another 150 feet, A.T. turns left.
3.4   Reach woods road. Turn left and follow road, with Island Pond visible just below through trees. (To right, woods road leads to Arden Valley Road in 0.6 mile.)
3.5   Turn right off woods road, and cross brook, entering hemlock woods.
3.7   Make short ascent followed by short descent, then cross brook.
4.1   Pass fern-topped boulder on right, propped up by small stone, and descend steadily through hemlocks.
4.5   Cross intermittent stream, then begin to descend.
4.7   Ascend gradually, then turn right, and descend.
5.2   Turn right onto woods road, then turn sharp left at fork. (Road straight ahead leads to abandoned cabin at southern end of Island Pond). Pass through swampy area, which is outlet of Island Pond.
5.4   Turn left, leaving woods road, which continues along west shore of Island Pond 1.0 mile to Arden Valley Road. Pass through mountain-laurel thickets.
5.5   Pass through grassy area.
5.6   Cross outlet of swamp, and begin gradual ascent to ridge of Green Pond Mountain.
5.7   Cross ridge of Green Pond Mountain, with views (when trees are bare) right (west) toward Indian Hill, then descend.
5.8   Descend very steeply over rocky ridge.
6.0   Pass through rocky area.
6.2   Turn right to cross stream, then right again to join green-blazed trail that comes in from left. This is an unofficial trail to Island Pond and is not maintained. In 250 feet, green-blazed trail leaves to right.

6.5   Turn sharp left, cross stream, then turn right, and continue along stream.

6.7   Turn right on Old Arden Road (woods road that once connected the Arden estate of the Harriman family with Tuxedo, now destroyed in part by the construction of the N.Y. State Thruway). Skirt the Elk Pen Field to the left. This field, with pieces of metal fence, is all that remains of an unsuccessful attempt by the Harrimans to establish an elk herd here.

7.1   Reach paved Arden Valley Road. Turn left, and follow road. A-SB Trail runs concurrently with A.T. along road.

7.2   Pass entrance to Elk Pen parking lot on left.

7.3   Cross N.Y. State Thruway and railroad tracks on overpass, and continue along road, passing stone building (ranger's house) to left.

7.5   Reach N.Y. 17 (end of section). To continue, cross road, and reenter woods (see New York Section Twelve).

Trail Description, South to North

Miles   **Data**

0.0   From N.Y. 17, proceed east on paved Arden Valley Road.

0.2   Cross railroad tracks and N.Y. State Thruway on overpass. At this point, the A.T. runs concurrently with the Arden-Surebridge (A-SB) Trail (red-triangle-on-white blazes).

0.3   Pass entrance to Elk Pen parking lot on right.

0.4   Turn right on chained-off woods road (Old Arden Road), skirting the Elk Pen Field to the right. A-SB Trail continues ahead on paved road. Old Arden Road formerly connected the Arden estate of the Harriman family with Tuxedo but was destroyed in part by construction of N.Y. State Thruway. Metal fence around field is all that remains of the Harrimans' unsuccessful attempt to establish an elk herd here.

0.8   Turn left into woods, and begin to ascend.

0.9   Turn left to cross stream. Continue winding, gradual ascent.

1.2   After short descent, reach junction with green-blazed trail that enters from left and begins to run concurrently with A.T. This is an unofficial trail to Island Pond and is not maintained.

1.3   Turn left, leaving green-blazed trail, cross stream, and continue uphill through hemlocks, soon passing through rocky area.

1.6   Turn left to climb very steeply over rocky ridge.

1.8   Cross ridge of Green Pond Mountain, with views (when trees are bare) left (west) toward Indian Hill. Descend slightly to cross outlet of swamp, then pass through hemlock grove.

2.0   Pass through grassy area, then continue through mountain-laurel thickets.

2.1   Trail turns right on woods road and follows it east through second swamp, which is outlet of Island Pond. (To left, this road goes north along west shore of Island Pond 1.0 mile to Arden Valley Road.)

2.3   Bear right at fork in road. (Left fork leads to abandoned cabin at southern end of Island Pond.) Shortly turn left into woods, ascending gradually.

2.7   Turn left, and descend gradually, soon passing through hemlocks.

3.0   Cross intermittent stream, soon beginning to ascend.

3.4   Skirt fern-topped boulder, propped up by small stone, to left, then descend through hemlocks.

3.7   Cross brook, and make short ascent followed by short descent.

4.0   Cross brook, then turn left on woods road. To left, through trees, Island Pond is visible just below.

4.1   Turn right into woods, leaving woods road, which continues ahead to reach Arden Valley Road in 0.6 mile.

4.3   Reach the Lemon Squeezer, a narrow, steep passage between large boulders. The Arden-Surebridge (A-SB) Trail, with red-triangle-on-white blazes, comes in from right, and both trails climb together through this formation, approximately 300 feet to the top. If climb is too steep, use bypass trail to left. From top of Lemon Squeezer, Trail ascends gradually up Island Pond Mountain.

4.6   Reach summit of Island Pond Mountain (1,303 feet). Trail turns right and begins to descend. (A-SB Trail continues straight ahead, reaching Arden Valley Road in about 0.4 mile.)

5.0   Cross blue-blazed Long Path.

5.1   Turn left, following left bank of intermittent stream, then cross stream, and continue along right bank of stream.

5.2   Turn right, leaving stream, and ascend steeply.

5.5   Reach height of land on Surebridge Mountain, and begin to descend.

5.8   Cross Surebridge Brook, and turn left onto Surebridge Mine Road (also known as Lost Road). Pass Greenwood Mine to right of Trail, now a water-filled pit. During the Civil War, iron ore from this mine was hauled to the Greenwood Furnace in Arden.

5.9   Turn right, and begin steep ascent through hemlocks.

6.4   Reach ridge of Fingerboard Mountain, and turn left as red-on-white-blazed Ramapo-Dunderberg (R-D) Trail comes in from right and joins A.T.

6.5   Blue-blazed Hurst Trail on right leads to **Fingerboard Shelter**, visible immediately below, and in 0.5 mile to Seven Lakes Drive at south end of Lake Tiorati. This trail was named for Harvey Hurst, a member of the Green Mountain Club, who opened the trail in 1922.

7.0   Reach summit of Fingerboard Mountain (1,328 feet), marked by stone fireplace to left of Trail. Begin to descend.

7.4   Pass under telephone wires, and join woods road, with round water tank to right.

7.5   Reach paved Arden Valley Road (end of section). To continue, cross road and follow Trail north into woods (see New York Section Ten).

N.Y. 17 (Arden) to N.Y. 17A (Mt. Peter)
New York Section Twelve
11.9 Miles

Brief Description of Section

This section of the A.T. is in woods, except for four road crossings: Orange Turnpike, East Mombasha Road, West Mombasha Road, and Lakes Road. It includes a traverse of four mountains: Arden Mountain, Buchanan Mountain, Mombasha High Point, and Bellvale Mountain. Elevation at N.Y. 17 is 500 feet and at N.Y. 17A, 1,130 feet. The highest elevation is 1,294 feet, at Bellvale Mountain.

Circular depressions on the forest floor are former charcoal burning pits where hemlock was converted to charcoal for smelting iron ore. Harvesting the timber needed for the charcoal virtually denuded the hills. The forest the hiker sees today is mostly secondary growth. Brooks and streams in this area are often colored brown as a result of iron salts leaching through the soil.

Road Approaches

Both the northern and southern ends of this section are accessible by vehicle. At the northern end, the Trail crosses N.Y. 17, 0.7 mile south of Arden, at Arden Valley Road, which enters Harriman State Park to the east. Parking is available on the east (northbound) side of N.Y. 17, 0.1 mile north of Arden Valley Road. Additional parking space is available at the Elk Pen parking lot on Arden Valley Road, 0.3 mile east of its intersection with N.Y. 17. Drivers approaching this end of the Trail via the New York Thruway should note that the closest exits onto N.Y. 17 are at Harriman to the north (exit 16) and at Suffern to the south (exit 15).

At the southern end, the Trail crosses N.Y. 17A at Mt. Peter, 2.0 miles north of the village of Greenwood Lake and 1.6 miles east of Bellvale. Parking is available on the paved strip of the old highway (known as Continental Road) around which the improved N.Y. 17A has been built.

Road access is also available at Orange Turnpike (1.8 miles from the northern end of the section), East Mombasha Road (3.2 miles from the northern end of the section), West Mombasha Road (5.0 miles from the northern end of the section), and Lakes Road (3.6 miles from the southern end of the section). No parking is available at Orange Turnpike or West Mombasha Road. Limited parking is available at East Mombasha Road and Lakes Road, but overnight parking is not permitted.

Public Transportation

The northern end of this section can be reached from New York City and local points to the north by Short Line bus, (212) 736-4700. A flag stop will be made on request at the Trail crossing at Arden Valley Road, and scheduled stops are made at the Red Apple Rest in Southfields, 2.1 miles south of the A.T. on N.Y. 17.

The southern end of this section can be reached from New York City and from Warwick, New York, by New Jersey Transit buses (Route No. 196-197), (201) 762-5100. A flag stop will be made at Mt. Peter (Kain Road), 0.2 mile west of the A.T. on N.Y. 17A.

Maps

For route navigation, refer to Map Three with this guide. For area detail, refer to the following USGS 7 1/2-minute topographic quadrangles: Monroe, New York; Warwick, New York; Greenwood Lake, New York-New Jersey.

Shelters and Campsites

No shelters or campsites are available in this section.

Supplies and Services

At the northern end of this section, meals may be obtained at the Red Apple Rest in Southfields, 2.1 miles south of the A.T. on N.Y. 17. A deli, with a limited selection of groceries, is 1.8 miles south of Trail crossing. The nearest post office is at Arden (ZIP Code 10910), 0.7 mile north of the A.T. on N.Y. 17. (Post office is in former Arden railroad station, 0.2 mile east of N.Y. 17 on secondary road.) A post office is at Southfields (ZIP Code 10975), too. A larger selection of groceries is available in Tuxedo, 5.5 miles to the south on N.Y. 17. A public telephone is located at the Trail crossing of N.Y. 17.

The southern end has a grocery store and post office (ZIP Code 10912) at Bellvale, 1.6 miles west of the A.T. on N.Y. 17A. A variety of supplies and services, including restaurants, a supermarket, and a post office (ZIP Code 10925), is available at Greenwood Lake, 2.0 miles south of the A.T. on N.Y. 17A and N.Y. 210.

Public Accommodations

The northern end of this section has a motel at Southfields, 2.1 miles south of the A.T. on N.Y. 17. At the southern end, tourist homes are available in Greenwood Lake, 2.0 miles south of the A.T. on N.Y. 17A and N.Y. 210, and motels are available in Warwick, 3.5 miles to the west along N.Y. 17A.

Trail Description, North to South

Miles	Data
0.0	From west side of N.Y. 17 at Arden Valley Road, proceed west, entering woods on footpath. Soon begin steep (very steep in places) climb of Agony Grind.
0.2	Blue-blazed trail bypasses very steep ascent of rock.
0.4	Reach viewpoint to east over Ramapo Valley and N.Y. State Thruway, with Harriman State Park beyond. Grade moderates.
0.8	Trail register is on tree to left of Trail. Please sign.
0.9	Reach brush-covered area, with limited view back over Ramapo Valley to Harriman State Park, then descend briefly.
1.1	Reach scrub oak-covered summit of Arden Mountain (1,180 feet), with limited views west and north. Trail descends through hemlock grove.

1.5	After brief ascent, reach secondary peak, with views to west. Begin to descend.
1.6	Rocky ledges allow views west to Mombasha High Point and Bellvale Mountain and north to Catskill Mountains on the horizon. Trail continues to descend.
1.8	Reach paved Orange Turnpike. A pipe spring, a water source, is 0.5 mile south of Trail crossing on east side of road, by a gravel pull-off area beyond a dip in road. Trail turns left along road for 250 feet, crosses road, and reenters woods, climbing steeply through hemlocks.
2.0	Trail levels off.
2.1	At viewpoint to left, turn right, and begin to descend through hemlock grove.
2.2	Trail levels off.
2.5	Reach eastern end of Little Dam Lake. Trail passes around northern side of lake, which is visible to left of Trail.
2.9	Cross wood-truss bridge over inlet of Little Dam Lake.
3.0	Trail continues on old, winding woods road.
3.2	Reach paved East Mombasha Road. Cross road, and reenter woods on footpath, ascending steadily.
3.4	Reach viewpoint to east over Little Dam Lake at secondary summit of Buchanan Mountain, then steeply descend rocky, hemlock-covered slope.
3.5	Cross stream.
3.6	Cross second stream.
3.7	After descent, cross third stream. In 200 feet, cross fourth stream, and begin steady ascent.
4.0	Reach beautiful viewpoint near summit of Buchanan Mountain (1,142 feet).
4.2	Trail runs along edge of escarpment.
4.3	Turn left, and descend steeply over jumbled rocks.
4.5	After passing through hemlock grove and mountain-laurel thicket, cross stream, and ascend briefly.
4.7	Turn right, and descend rocky slope.
4.8	Cross stream.
4.9	Reach paved West Mombasha Road. Turn left, and follow road.
5.0	Turn right, cross road, cross bridge over ditch, and follow posts across field.

5.1   Reach end of field, and continue on old woods road.

5.3   Pass through gap in stone wall, then ascend steeply. Turn right at top of ascent.

5.5   Cross grassy woods road, and continue to ascend.

5.7   Turn left onto dirt road and pass through gap in stone wall. Continue straight ahead on footpath as dirt road curves to right. Trail ascends gradually.

6.0   After steep ascent, reach Mombasha High Point (1,280 feet). Mombasha Lake is visible below (to left), with Schunemunk Mountain behind it to the northeast. Kloiber's Pond is straight ahead (along road). Harriman State Park is visible to the east, and, on a clear day, New York City may be seen on the horizon, due magnetic south. To the west is the ridge of Bellvale Mountain.

6.8   Blue-blazed Allis Trail branches off to left and descends over One Cedar Mountain to N.Y. 17A. This trail is named for banker J. Ashton Allis, a pioneer trail builder, for many years president of Fresh Air Club, and an early treasurer of ATC. A viewpoint is at 100 feet on Allis Trail, with High Point Monument and relay towers and Mt. Tammany at Delaware Water Gap visible to west. A.T. makes sharp right turn and descends.

6.9   Trail levels off.

7.0   Make sharp right turn.

7.6   Pass old stone walls, remains of an abandoned settlement, to right of Trail.

7.8   Cross dirt road, then cross tributary stream.

7.9   Cross a tributary of Trout Brook, then cross the brook.

8.0   Reach top of Fitzgerald Falls, a 25-foot waterfall in a rocky cleft. Turn left, and steeply descend on rock steps along left side of falls. At base of falls, turn right, crossing the brook, and continue along the brook. Blue-blazed bypass trail going straight ahead through hemlock grove avoids two crossings of brook and frequently flooded area, rejoining A.T. in 0.1 mile.

8.3   After passing through area cleared for powerline, cross Trout Brook. In 75 feet, turn left off grassy road, and ascend on footpath to paved Lakes Road (Monroe Road). Cross road, and reenter woods, soon beginning to ascend Bellvale Mountain.

8.7	After steep ascent, make sharp left turn, and ascend more gradually.
8.9	Turn left onto old woods road (now merely a footpath), continuing to ascend gradually.
9.4	Trail levels off, then begins to descend.
9.6	Cross old stone wall.
9.8	Blue-blazed trail to right leads 450 feet to spring, a water source, and to well and hand pump, which provide water in dry seasons. In 225 feet after junction of A.T. with side trail to spring, cross small brook.
10.1	Climb to top of Cat Rocks, an upturned strata of reddish conglomerate (puddingstone) with top leveled by glacial action. Views to the east and south. Blue-blazed trail to right bypasses steep climb and rejoins A.T. in 275 feet.
10.3	Cross brook.
10.5	Leave woods, and cross rocky area.
10.6	Reach top of Eastern Pinnacles, another conglomerate outcropping, with good views north, east, and south over Greenwood Lake. Blue-blazed trail to right bypasses steep descent and rejoins A.T. in 150 feet. Descend steeply from rocks and continue along grassy road, soon beginning gradual ascent.
10.8	Trail levels off.
11.2	Cross cleared utility right-of-way.
11.5	Continue on footpath as woods road curves off to right.
11.9	Reach N.Y. 17A. Turn right, and follow road for 150 feet, then take left fork onto old road (Continental Road). Continue on Continental Road for 150 feet until Trail turns left and reenters woods on footpath (end of section) (see New York Section Thirteen).

Trail Description, South to North

Miles   **Data**

0.0	Proceed east along Continental Road for 150 feet to its intersection with N.Y. 17A, then cross to northern side

of N.Y. 17A. Turn right, and follow road for 150 feet, then turn left, and enter woods on footpath.

0.4   Join woods road coming in from left, and continue on woods road.

0.7   Cross cleared utility right-of-way.

1.1   Trail begins to descend gradually.

1.3   Climb steeply to top of Eastern Pinnacles, an upturned strata of reddish conglomerate (puddingstone), with good views north, east, and south over Greenwood Lake Valley. Blue-blazed trail to left bypasses steep climb and rejoins A.T. in 150 feet.

1.6   Cross brook.

1.8   Climb to top of Cat Rocks, another conglomerate outcropping with top leveled by glacial action. Views to the east and south. Blue-blazed trail to right bypasses steep climb and rejoins A.T. in 275 feet.

2.1   Cross small brook. In another 225 feet, blue-blazed trail to left leads 450 feet to spring, a water source, and to well and hand pump, which provide water in dry seasons. Trail begins to ascend.

2.3   Cross old stone wall. Trail continues to ascend.

2.5   Trail levels off, then descends gradually.

3.0   Turn right, ascend briefly, then continue to descend.

3.2   Make sharp right turn at double blaze, and begin steeper descent.

3.6   Reach paved Lakes Road (Monroe Road). Cross road, descend on footpath, briefly turn right on grassy road, and cross Trout Brook. Pass through area cleared for powerline.

3.8   Cross brook again, then turn left, and continue along brook through hemlock grove. Blue-blazed bypass trail bears right and ascends through hemlocks, avoiding two additional crossings of brook and area frequently flooded. Bypass trail rejoins A.T. in 0.1 mile at base of falls.

3.9   Reach base of Fitzgerald Falls, a 25-foot waterfall in a rocky cleft. Cross stream just below falls, and ascend steeply on rock steps along right side of falls.

4.0   Cross stream and tributary stream, and pass through hemlock grove.

4.1   Cross tributary stream again, then cross dirt road, and continue to ascend.

4.3   Pass stone walls, remains of an abandoned settlement, to left of Trail.

4.9   Make sharp left turn.

5.0   Begin steady ascent.

5.1   At top of rise, blue-blazed Allis Trail branches off to right and descends over One Cedar Mountain to N.Y. 17A. This trail is named for banker J. Ashton Allis, a pioneer trail builder, for many years president of Fresh Air Club, and an early treasurer of ATC. A viewpoint is in 100 feet on Allis Trail, with High Point Monument and relay towers and Mt. Tammany at Delaware Water Gap visible to west. A.T. levels off.

5.9   Reach Mombasha High Point (1,280 feet). Mombasha Lake is visible below (to left), with Schunemunk Mountain behind it to the northeast. Kloiber's Pond is straight ahead (along road). Harriman State Park is visible to the east, and, on a clear day, New York City may be seen on the horizon, due magnetic south. To the west is the ridge of Bellvale Mountain. Trail descends steeply, then more gradually.

6.2   Join dirt road that comes in from left. In another 100 feet, pass through gap in stone wall, then turn right, leaving dirt road, and continue on footpath.

6.4   After descent, cross grassy woods road.

6.6   Turn left, descend steeply, then pass through gap in stone wall, and continue on old woods road.

6.8   Emerge onto overgrown field. Follow posts across field.

6.9   Cross bridge over ditch, and reach paved West Mombasha Road. Turn left, and follow road.

7.0   Turn right, cross road, and reenter woods.

7.1   Cross stream. In 200 feet, turn left, ascending rocky slope.

7.4   After brief descent, cross stream, then pass through mountain-laurel thicket and hemlock grove.

7.6   Ascend steeply over jumbled rocks, then turn right, and follow edge of escarpment.

7.9	Reach viewpoint near summit of Buchanan Mountain (1,142 feet). Begin steady descent.
8.2	Cross stream. In 200 feet, cross second stream, and ascend.
8.3	Cross third stream.
8.4	Cross fourth stream, then steeply ascend rocky slope.
8.5	Reach second summit of Buchanan Mountain, with view to east over Little Dam Lake. Begin to descend.
8.7	Reach paved East Mombasha Road. Cross road, and continue on old, winding woods road.
8.9	Woods road narrows into footpath.
9.0	Cross wood-truss bridge over inlet of Little Dam Lake. Trail passes around north shore of lake, which is visible to right of Trail.
9.4	Reach east end of lake.
9.7	Begin moderately steep ascent through hemlock grove.
9.8	Turn left at top of ascent, with views to left.
9.9	Begin descent through hemlock grove.
10.1	After steeper descent, reach paved Orange Turnpike. A pipe spring, a water source, is 0.5 mile south of Trail crossing on the east side of the road, by a gravel pull-off area beyond a dip in the road. Trail turns left along road for 250 feet, then crosses road, and reenters woods, beginning ascent of Arden Mountain.
10.3	Rocky ledges allow views west to Mombasha High Point and Bellvale Mountain and north to Catskill Mountains on the horizon. Trail continues to ascend.
10.4	Reach secondary peak. Begin to descend.
10.6	Ascend steadily through hemlock grove.
10.8	Reach scrub oak-covered summit of Arden Mountain (1,180 feet), with limited views west and north.
11.0	After brief ascent, reach brush-covered area.
11.1	Trail register is on tree to right of Trail. Please sign.
11.5	At viewpoint to east over Ramapo Valley and N.Y. State Thruway, with Harriman State Park beyond, begin steep (very steep in places) descent of Agony Grind.
11.7	Blue-blazed trail bypasses very steep descent of rock.
11.9	Reach N.Y. 17 at its intersection with Arden Valley Road (end of section). To continue, cross N.Y. 17, and continue east on Arden Valley Road (see New York Section Eleven).

N.Y. 17A (Mt. Peter) to New York-New Jersey State Line
New York Section Thirteen
5.9 Miles

Brief Description of Section

The Trail in this section follows the ridge of Bellvale Mountain, with many beautiful views over Greenwood Lake and the Ramapo hills from open ledges. Although there is little change in elevation from the northern end of the section at N.Y. 17A (1,130 feet) to the southern end at the state line (about 1,350 feet), the route has many short, steep ascents and descents along the crest of the ridge. The highest point is at Prospect Rock (1,433 feet). Blue-blazed side trails descend from the A.T. to N.Y. 210 at several points along the section. The Trail passes through oak and hickory forests, with pitch pine on the rocky ledges.

Road Approaches

At the northern end of the section, the Trail crosses N.Y. 17A at Mt. Peter, 2.0 miles north of the village of Greenwood Lake and 1.6 miles east of Bellvale. The northern end of the section starts at Continental Road, the paved strip of the old highway around which the improved N.Y. 17A has been built. Ample parking is available along Continental Road at the Trail crossing.

The southern end of the section is at the New York-New Jersey state boundary. The nearest road access to this point is from N.Y. 210, which runs along the shore of Greenwood Lake. The State Line Trail (see description at end of section) ascends from opposite the Greenwood Lake Marina on N.Y. 210 and follows the state line for 1.2 miles until it reaches the A.T. on the crest of Bellvale Mountain. Parking for two to three cars may be available at the intersection of N.Y. 210 with Lake Shore Drive, immediately north of the Greenwood Lake Marina. Parking is not permitted at the marina.

Public Transportation

Both the northern and southern ends of this section can be reached from New York City and from Warwick, New York, by New Jersey Transit buses (Route No. 196-197), (201) 762-5100. At the northern end, a flag stop will be made on request at Mt. Peter (Kain Road), 0.2 mile west of the Trail crossing on N.Y. 17A. A flag stop will also be made at the junction of the State Line Trail and N.Y. 210 at the Greenwood Lake Marina, 1.2 miles from the southern end of the section via the State Line Trail.

Maps

For route navigation, refer to Maps Three and Four with this guide. For area detail, refer to the following USGS 7 1/2-minute topographic quadrangle: Greenwood Lake, New York-New Jersey. Another reference is NY-NJ TC Trail Map No. 21 (North Jersey Trails-Western Portion).

Shelters and Campsites

No shelters or campsites are available in this section.

Supplies and Services

The northern end of this section has a grocery store and post office (ZIP Code 10912) at Bellvale, 1.6 miles west of the A.T. on N.Y. 17A. A wide variety of supplies and services, including restaurants, a supermarket, and a post office (ZIP Code 10925), is available in the village of Greenwood Lake. From the northern end of the section, Greenwood Lake is 2.0 miles to the south via N.Y. 17A and 210. The village can also be reached via the Mountain Spring Trail, which leaves the A.T. 1.8 miles from the northern end of the section (descend 0.5 mile to N.Y. 210, then follow N.Y. 210 to the north for 0.4 mile to traffic light at center of village). At the southern end of the section, meals may be obtained at the Lakeside Inn, 1.1 miles south of the terminus of the State Line Trail on County 511 (the continuation in New Jersey of N.Y. 210).

Public Accommodations

Tourist homes are located in Greenwood Lake, 2.0 miles south of the northern end of this section, and motels in Warwick, 3.5 miles to the west along N.Y. 17A. A motel is located on County 511 (the continuation in New Jersey of N.Y. 210) 1.8 miles south of the terminus of the State Line Trail. Another motel is on N.Y. 210, 0.2 mile south of the terminus of the Mountain Spring Trail, which leaves the A.T. 1.8 miles from the northern end of the section.

Trail Description, North to South

Miles	Data
0.0	From paved Continental Road, turn south, and enter woods. Cross woods road, and ascend.
0.5	At clearing for powerlines, Trail curves to left, then right, and passes over rocks. Good views to north and east from top of rocks.
0.8	With telephone lines overhead, cross brook, which is outlet of marsh to right of Trail.
1.8	Blue-blazed Mountain Spring Trail leaves to left and descends 0.5 mile to N.Y. 210. (See description of trail at end of section.)
2.0	At rock painted with "W," unmarked Mother Rialto Trail descends to right, with spring to left of trail 225 yards downhill.
2.2	Emerge onto an exposed section of the ridge, with beautiful views of Greenwood Lake to east.
2.5	Descend steeply to cross small brook.
2.9	After passing through clearing, cross Cascade Brook, and ascend through hemlocks.
3.1	Trail ascends to viewpoint.
3.3	Descend to brook in hollow, then ascend, crossing brook several times.
3.4	Emerge again onto open rocks, with good views to east over Greenwood Lake. Ascend briefly, then come out once more on exposed rocks, with more views.

3.7   Blue-blazed trail descends to left for 0.3 mile to residential streets in Indian Park, which lead in another 0.5 mile to N.Y. 210.

3.9   Reach rock outcrop, with 360-degree view. Continue along open rocks on east side of ridge, with views of Greenwood Lake below.

4.3   Descend very steeply, then cross old road, and turn left.

4.5   Cross Furnace Brook, a source of water.

4.9   Begin gradual ascent.

5.3   After steep climb, turn sharp left. To right, rocky promontory provides beautiful views west, north, and east. In another 150 feet, turn left again.

5.4   Reach Prospect Rock (1,433 feet), with magnificent views over Greenwood Lake to east and Taylor and Warwick mountains to west.

5.5   Reach trail register on tree to right of Trail (please sign), then turn left at A.T. survey marker.

5.7   Beautiful views to west from open rocks.

5.9   Reach blue-blazed State Line Trail at New York-New Jersey state line (end of section). (See below for description of this trail.) To continue, proceed straight ahead on A.T (see New Jersey Section One).

Trail Description, South to North

Miles   **Data**

0.0   From intersection of blue-blazed State Line Trail at New Jersey-New York state line, proceed north on footpath.

0.1   Beautiful views to west from open rocks.

0.4   At A.T. survey marker, turn right, and reach trail register on tree to left of Trail (please sign). After short climb, reach Prospect Rock (1,433 feet). Magnificent views over Greenwood Lake to east and Taylor and Warwick mountains to west.

0.6   Turn right, and cross to east side of ridge. In another 150 feet, make sharp right, and descend, first steeply then more gradually. Before second turn, rocky promontory directly ahead provides beautiful views west, north, and east.

1.3   Cross Furnace Brook, a source of water.

1.6   After crossing old road, climb steeply, then very steeply, reaching viewpoint to south, east, and west. Trail follows crest of ridge for next 0.4 mile, with many good views of Greenwood Lake below.

2.1   Blue-blazed trail descends to right for 0.3 mile to reach residential streets in Indian Park, which lead in another 0.5 mile to N.Y. 210.

2.4   Trail again comes out on open rocks, with good views to east over Greenwood Lake. Descend briefly, then come out once more on exposed rocks, with more views.

2.5   Turn sharp left, and begin to descend, crossing small brook several times, then ascend gradually.

2.8   Trail begins to descend.

3.0   After descending through hemlocks, cross Cascade Brook, and pass through clearing, then ascend briefly.

3.4   Cross small brook, then ascend steeply.

3.5   Reach viewpoint over Greenwood Lake. Continue along ridge, with more views of lake below.

3.7   Turn left, away from exposed ridge, and enter woods on grassy footpath.

3.9   At rock painted with "W," unmarked Mother Rialto Trail descends to left, with spring to left of trail 225 yards downhill.

4.1   Blue-blazed Mountain Spring Trail leaves to right and descends 0.5 mile to N.Y. 210. (See description of trail at end of section.)

5.1   With telephone lines overhead, cross brook, which is outlet of marsh to left of Trail.

5.4   At clearing for powerlines, Trail passes over rocks and curves to left, then to right. Good views to north and east from top of rocks.

5.9   Reach paved Continental Road (end of section). To continue, turn right along road, and continue along N.Y. 17A, which comes in from left, then turn left and enter woods (see New York Section Twelve).

State Line Trail

This blue-blazed trail descends from the A.T., following the New York-New Jersey state line, to N.Y. 210 opposite the Greenwood Lake Marina. From its junction with the A.T. at the southern end of this section, it proceeds east, crossing the ridge of Bellvale Mountain, with numerous short ascents and descents. At 0.4 mile, the trail turns sharply to the right, then immediately to the left, and starts steady descent. The yellow-blazed Ernest Walter Trail, which makes loop around Surprise Lake and West Pond, turns off to right at 0.5 mile. At 0.7 mile, log steps along trail prevent erosion. With houses in view to right at 0.9 mile, trail turns left and continues descent, reaching N.Y. 210 opposite the Greenwood Lake Marina at 1.2 mile.

Mountain Spring Trail

This trail, also blue-blazed, descends from the A.T. at a point 1.8 miles from the northern end of the section and, in 0.5 mile, reaches N.Y. 210. The trail begins by descending on a moderate grade. At 0.2 mile, the trail descends more steeply, as an unmarked side trail turns off to the right. The trail joins a woods road at 0.3 mile and continues descending along this road until it reaches N.Y. 210 at 0.5 mile. A public telephone is located at the junction of the trail with N.Y. 210, which is immediately south of Andy's Alignment Service. From this point, the village of Greenwood Lake is 0.4 mile to the north along N.Y. 210. A motel and a restaurant are located 0.2 mile south on N.Y. 210.

New York-New Jersey State Line to N.J. 94
New Jersey Section One
10.1 Miles

Brief Description of Section

This section begins at the New York-New Jersey state line along the ridge of Bearfort Mountain, west of Greenwood Lake. The Trail follows the ridge for about 0.3 mile, passing through Abram S. Hewitt State Forest, then turns right, and begins to run in a generally northwesterly direction. After crossing Warwick Turnpike, it traverses Wawayanda State Park. Wawayanda is the name given by the Lenape Indians to a creek they called "water on the mountain." The Trail passes through an upland deciduous forest, with some red cedar, hemlock, and rhododendron.

Road Approaches

Only the southern end of this section is directly accessible by vehicle. The southern end is at the intersection of N.J. 94 and Maple Grange Road, about 1.5 miles north of Vernon. Parking for four or five cars is available in a dirt turnout just north of the Trail crossing.

The northern end of the section is at the New York-New Jersey state boundary. The nearest road access to this point is from N.Y. 210, which runs along the shore of Greenwood Lake. The State Line Trail (see description at end of New York Section 13) ascends from opposite the Greenwood Lake Marina on N.Y. 210 and follows the state line for 1.2 miles until it reaches the A.T. on the crest of Bellvale Mountain. Parking for two to three cars may be available at the intersection of N.Y. 210 with Lake Shore Drive, immediately north of the Greenwood Lake Marina. Parking is not permitted at the marina.

In addition, road access is available at Long House Road (Brady Road), 2.2 miles from the northern end of the section, and at Warwick Turnpike, 3.6 miles from the northern end. Limited parking is available at the Trail crossing of Long House Road. No parking is available at Warwick Turnpike, but ample parking is available at the headquarters of Wawayanda State Park, located off Warwick Turnpike about 0.3 mile south of the Trail crossing. A blue-blazed side trail links the park headquarters with the A.T., 3.9 miles from the northern end of the section.

Public Transportation

The State Line Trail, leading to the northern end of this section, can be reached from New York City and Warwick, New York, by New Jersey Transit buses (Route No. 196-197), (201) 762-5100. A flag stop can be requested for the junction of the State Line Trail and N.Y. 210 at the Greenwood Lake Marina. No public transportation is available at the southern end of the section.

Maps

For route navigation, refer to Map Four with this guide. For area detail, refer to the following USGS 7 1/2-minute topographic quadrangles: Greenwood Lake, New York-New Jersey; Wawayanda, New Jersey-New York. Another reference is NY-NJ TC Trail Map No. 21 (North Jersey Trails-Western Portion).

Shelters and Campsites

One campsite, maintained by Wawayanda State Park for thru-hikers, is available 4.1 miles from the northern end of the section and 6.0 miles from the southern end of the section; water at park headquarters, 0.5 mile from campsite (reached via blue-blazed side trail).

Supplies and Services

At the northern end of the section, meals may be obtained at the Lakeside Inn, 1.1 miles south of the terminus of the State Line Trail on County 511 (the continuation in New Jersey of N.Y. 210). At the southern end, groceries, a pharmacy, and a post office (ZIP Code 07462) are available in Vernon, 1.5 miles south of the Trail crossing along N.J. 94. In addition, meals are available at restaurants along Warwick Turnpike, both 0.7 mile north and 1.6 miles south of the

Trail crossing, and a shopping center is at the junction of N.Y. 94 and Warwick Turnpike, 2.4 miles north of the Trail crossing of Warwick Turnpike. A deli, with groceries, is located on Warwick Turnpike, 1.9 miles south of the Trail crossing.

Public Accommodations

At the northern end of the section, a motel is located along County 511 (the continuation in New Jersey of N.Y. 210) 1.8 miles south of the terminus of the State Line Trail on N.Y. 210. At the southern end of the section, the Appalachian Motel is located along N.J. 94, 0.6 mile south of the Trail crossing. In addition, lodging may be obtained at the Willow Brook Inn, 0.7 mile north of the Trail crossing of Warwick Turnpike.

Trail Description, North to South

Miles	Data
0.0	From junction with State Line Trail, continue south on A.T.
0.2	Reach viewpoint to east over Surprise Lake and Sterling Ridge, and begin to descend.
0.3	A.T. turns right as yellow-blazed Ernest Walter Trail continues straight ahead. Ernest Walter Trail makes loop around West Pond and Surprise Lake and connects in about 1.0 mile with the white-blazed Bearfort Ridge Trail, which leads 2.5 miles south to Warwick Turnpike.
0.5	Reach rock ledge, with view to west.
0.7	Cross small stream on rocks.
0.8	Cross woods road. In 450 feet, cross another woods road.
1.0	Turn left onto dirt road for 45 feet, then turn right, and continue to descend.
1.1	Cross Long House Creek on split-log bridge.
1.5	Cross stream on log bridge.
1.7	Turn right onto woods road for 35 feet, then turn left, and reenter woods.

1.9	Turn right onto grassy woods road.
2.0	Turn left, and reenter woods.
2.2	Reach paved Long House Road (Brady Road). Turn left, and follow road for 375 feet, then turn right, and reenter woods.
2.3	Turn right onto old woods road for 40 feet, then turn left, and cross intermittent stream on logs.
2.5	Ascend steeply under hemlock tree.
2.6	Make sharp left turn.
2.9	Cross old woods road.
3.1	Cross brook.
3.2	Ascend very steeply, with stone wall to right.
3.3	Join old farm road that comes in from left. In another 125 feet, road curves to left and continues along right side of overgrown field.
3.4	At end of field, bear left, and follow road along edge of field, then turn right, and reenter woods.
3.5	Turn left, and cross remains of old stone wall.
3.6	Cross paved Warwick Turnpike.
3.8	Cross plank bridge over outlet of swamp, and begin to ascend.
3.9	Turn right, and continue to ascend. In another 200 feet, join woods road coming in from left. (To left, blue-blazed trail leads 0.3 mile to headquarters of Wawayanda State Park.)
4.1	Designated **campsite** (for thru-hikers only) is to right of Trail.
4.2	Turn left on dirt Wawayanda Road.
4.4	Turn right onto woods road.
4.6	Reach crest of rise, and begin gradual descent.
4.8	Emerge onto overgrown field. Follow old farm road along right side of field.
4.9	Turn left on dirt Iron Mountain Road (not passable by car).
5.1	Cross iron bridge over stream. In another 75 feet, turn right on old woods road.
5.2	Pass cleared area to left of Trail.
5.5	Turn left, and reenter woods. In 125 feet, turn right, and cross stream.

5.7	Make sharp left turn.
6.0	Turn left onto woods road, and descend.
6.1	Turn left, and reenter woods. In another 300 feet, turn left again, and begin to ascend. To right, Adam and Eve Mountains and the Shawangunks are visible in the distance.
6.3	Reach crest of hill, and begin to descend.
6.5	Cross dirt Barrett Road, and ascend over knob.
6.6	Ascend briefly, then begin to descend.
7.1	Turn left, and begin to parallel stream. In 350 feet, cross another stream near small waterfall.
7.2	Turn left, away from stream, and begin to ascend.
7.3	With house in sight to left, begin to descend.
7.5	Cross stream. In 250 feet, bear right, cross another stream, and begin to ascend.
7.7	Cross old woods road, and begin short descent. In 150 feet, cross wide stone wall.
7.8	Cross another stone wall, and ascend. In 150 feet, turn left, pass through gap in stone wall, and make short descent.
7.9	Begin gradual ascent.
8.5	Begin gradual descent.
8.6	Cross stone wall, turn right, and ascend. In 200 feet, turn left, and reach crest of ridge of Wawayanda Mountain.
8.9	Trail comes out on exposed rocks, with beautiful views to west across Wallkill Valley and over Pochuck Mountain to the Kittatinnies.
9.1	Turn right, and begin to descend.
9.7	Emerge onto field. Turn left, and skirt east end of field.
9.8	Turn right, and follow hedgerow on left along south side of field (being careful not to disturb crops).
9.9	Turn left, crossing hedgerow, then turn right, and continue along hedgerow.
10.1	Reach N.J. 94 (end of section). To continue, proceed straight ahead on Maple Grange Road (see New Jersey Section Two).

Trail Description, South to North

Miles   **Data**

0.0   At intersection of Maple Grange Road and N.J. 94, proceed east, following hedgerow on left across fields (being careful not to disturb growing crops).

0.2   Turn left, crossing hedgerow, then turn right, and follow hedgerow to end of field.

0.3   Turn left, and skirt eastern end of field.

0.4   Turn right, and ascend into woods, beginning climb of Wawayanda Mountain.

1.0   Reach crest of ridge. Turn left, and follow crest.

1.2   Trail comes out on exposed rocks, with beautiful views to west across Wallkill Valley and over Pochuck Mountain to the Kittatinnies.

1.4   Turn right, leaving crest of ridge, and descend. In 200 feet, turn left, crossing stone wall, and ascend gradually, then descend.

2.3   After short ascent, pass through gap in stone wall, then immediately turn right, and descend. In 150 feet, cross another stone wall.

2.4   Cross wide stone wall, and begin short ascent. In 150 feet, cross old woods road, and soon begin to descend.

2.6   Cross stream, and bear left. In 250 feet, cross another stream, and begin to ascend.

2.8   With house in sight to right, begin to descend.

2.9   Begin to parallel stream.

3.0   Cross another stream near small waterfall. In 350 feet, turn right, away from stream, and begin to ascend.

3.5   Make short descent, then ascend over knob, and descend.

3.6   Cross dirt Barrett Road. In 300 feet, begin to ascend.

4.0   With fields in sight directly ahead (and views ahead of Adam and Eve Mountains and the Shawangunks in the distance), turn right, and continue along trail for 300 feet, then turn right again, and ascend on woods road.

4.1   At crest of hill, turn right, and reenter woods.

4.4	Make sharp right turn.
4.6	Cross stream, and turn left. In 125 feet, turn right on old woods road.
4.9	Pass cleared area to right of Trail.
5.0	Turn left on dirt Iron Mountain Road (not passable by car), and cross iron bridge over stream.
5.2	Turn right onto old farm road, and follow road along left side of overgrown field.
5.3	Reenter woods.
5.5	Reach crest of rise, and begin gradual descent.
5.7	Turn left onto dirt Wawayanda Road.
5.9	Turn right onto woods road.
6.0	Designated **campsite** (for thru-hikers only) is to left of Trail.
6.2	Bear left at fork in road, and begin to descend. To right, blue-blazed trail leads 0.3 mile to headquarters of Wawayanda State Park. In another 200 feet, turn left, and continue to descend.
6.3	Cross plank bridge over outlet of swamp.
6.5	Cross paved Warwick Turnpike.
6.6	Cross remains of old stone wall, and turn right.
6.7	Leave woods, turn left, and follow old farm road along left side of overgrown field.
6.8	Bear right at fork in road. In another 125 feet, continue straight ahead as road curves to right, and reenter woods.
6.9	Descend very steeply, with stone wall to left.
7.0	Cross brook.
7.2	Cross old woods road.
7.5	Make sharp right turn. In another 350 feet, descend steeply under hemlock tree.
7.8	Cross intermittent stream on logs, turn right onto old woods road for 40 feet, then turn left, and ascend into woods.
7.9	Reach paved Long House Road (Brady Road). Turn left, and follow road for 375 feet, then turn right, and reenter woods.
8.1	Turn right onto grassy woods road.

8.2	Turn left, and reenter woods.
8.4	Turn right onto woods road for 35 feet, then turn left, and reenter woods.
8.6	Cross stream on log bridge.
9.0	Cross Long House Creek on split-log bridge.
9.1	Turn left onto dirt road for 45 feet, then turn right, and ascend into woods.
9.2	Cross woods road. In 450 feet, cross another woods road.
9.4	Cross small stream on rocks.
9.6	Reach rock ledge with view to west.
9.8	At junction with yellow-blazed Ernest Walter Trail, A.T. turns left and continues along rock ledges. Ernest Walter Trail makes loop around West Pond and Surprise Lake and connects in about 1.0 mile with the white-blazed Bearfort Ridge Trail, which leads 2.5 miles south to Warwick Turnpike.
9.9	Reach crest of Bearfort Mountain, with views to east over Surprise Lake and Sterling Ridge.
10.1	Reach blue-blazed State Line Trail (end of section). (For description of this trail, see end of New York Section Thirteen). To continue, proceed straight ahead on A.T. (see New York Section Thirteen.)

N.J. 94 to N.J. 284 (Unionville, New York)
New Jersey Section Two
11.1 Miles

Brief Description of Section

This section of the Trail begins at the intersection of Maple Grange Road and N.J. 94. It passes through Vernon Valley along hard-surfaced roads, and follows woods roads and paths over Pochuck Mountain. It then passes through a sod farm, following the dikes, briefly follows a paved road across the Wallkill River, and continues through woods and farms.

This region exhibits the influence of glaciation, particularly in the mucky soils of Vernon Valley, a former glacial lake. Pochuck Mountain, a block of resistant metamorphic gneiss, stands as the high point and drainage divide between Vernon Valley and Kittatinny Valley.

The easterly portion of this section of the Trail is being relocated from the roads to a protected corridor acquired by the State of New Jersey. Be alert to the painted blazes, and, if they deviate from the printed Trail description, follow the blazes in preference to the printed data.

Portions of the Trail in this section still pass through private property. Please be respectful of the rights of the landowners who have generously allowed the Trail to be routed through their property pending the completion of the permanent route over the corridor acquired by the State of New Jersey.

Few dependable sources of potable water are available along this section, so plan to carry sufficient water.

Road Approaches

Both the northern and southern ends of this section are accessible by vehicle. The northern end of the section is at the intersection of

N.J. 94 and Maple Grange Road, about 1.5 miles north of Vernon. Parking for four or five cars is available in a dirt turnout just north of the Trail crossing. At the southern end, the Trail crosses N.J. 284, 0.9 mile south of the center of Unionville, New York. Parking for four or five cars is available in a dirt turnout just north of the Trail crossing.

Public Transportation

No public transportation is available to either end of this section.

Maps

For route navigation, refer to Map Four of this guide. For area detail, refer to the following USGS 7 1/2-minute topographic quadrangles: Wawayanda, New Jersey-New York; Hamburg, New Jersey; Unionville, New York-New Jersey.

Shelters and Campsites

No shelters or campsites are available in this section at this time. A shelter is planned for construction during 1989 on Pochuck Mountain, along a blue-blazed side trail.

Supplies and Services

At the northern end of this section, groceries, a pharmacy, and a post office (ZIP Code 07462) are available in Vernon, 1.5 miles south of the Trail crossing along N.J. 94. At the southern end of the section, groceries, sandwiches, and a post office (ZIP Code 10988) are available in Unionville, New York, on N.Y. 284, 0.9 mile north of the Trail crossing.

Public Accommodations

At the northern end of the section, the Appalachian Motel is 0.6 mile south of the Trail crossing along N.J. 94. No accommodations are available at the southern end of the section.

Trail Description, North to South

Miles   **Data**

0.0   From intersection of N.J. 94 and Maple Grange Road, proceed west on Maple Grange Road.

0.3   Cross railroad tracks.

0.7   Cross bridge over stream.

1.1   Cross one-lane bridge over stream.

1.7   Turn right onto County 517.

2.5   Turn left, cross stile over stone wall, and cross wet area on puncheons, then ascend slightly over rise.

2.6   Reach top of rise. Cross wet area on puncheons, and descend across open fields, following posts.

2.7   Reach end of field, reenter woods, and begin ascent.

3.0   Reach viewpoint to east over Wawayanda Mountain, then pass through stand of red cedars, and cross stone wall, continuing to ascend.

3.1   Trail levels off.

3.3   Begin to descend.

3.4   Cross old woods road.

3.5   Trail levels off.

3.7   Trail runs parallel to stone wall on right. Soon begin to ascend, crossing several stone walls.

4.0   Descend from shoulder of hill.

4.1   Cross field, and reach paved County 565. Cross road, and follow posts across field.

4.2   Cross wooden bridge over stream, then pass through gap in stone wall. Begin to ascend.

4.3   Pass through old field, now overgrown with red cedars, then bear right, and continue across field.

4.4   At end of field, turn left, and continue along right side of field, with tree line to right.

4.5   Turn right, and reenter woods. In another 150 feet, cross swampy area on puncheons, then cross stream on rocks.

4.7   Cross private dirt road.

5.0   Cross swampy area on puncheons.

5.3   Reach summit of Pochuck Mountain. Side trail to right leads 40 feet to viewpoint over west ridge of mountain. Begin to descend.

5.5   Cross private dirt road, and continue to descend. In another 250 feet, cross swampy area on puncheons as Trail levels off. Soon pass through hemlock grove.

5.6   Turn right as old Trail route comes in from the left.

5.7   Join old woods road, which comes in from the right. Follow road for 150 feet, then turn right, leaving road. Begin gradual ascent.

6.0   Reach beautiful overlook, with views west across Wallkill Valley to High Point and the Kittatinnies. Continue along crest of middle ridge of Pochuck Mountain.

6.1   Begin to descend, first gradually, then more steeply.

6.3   Turn left onto woods road for 30 feet, then turn right, and begin to ascend.

6.6   Reach summit of western ridge of Pochuck Mountain, and begin to descend on switchbacks.

7.2   Emerge onto open field. Continue across field, then cross stone wall and row of trees, and emerge onto overgrown field. Follow posts downhill across field.

7.3   Reach paved Wallkill Road (also known as Liberty Corners Road). Turn right, and follow road for 120 feet, then cross road, and reenter woods.

7.4   Follow puncheons for about 0.4 mile across wet area.

7.8   Ascend wooden steps and turn left onto dirt road (abandoned railroad right-of-way). Follow dirt road along east side of Liberty Sod Farms.

8.1   Turn right, and follow dike across sod farm.

8.4   Road makes jog to right, then to left, and continues along south side of sod farm.

8.6   Turn right, and continue on road along west side of sod farm.

9.3   Turn left onto paved Oil City Road.

9.6   Cross bridge over Wallkill River.

9.8   Turn left onto paved road leading into Carnegie Industries (private property).

10.0   Turn right, and reenter woods. In another 75 feet, cross bridge over small stream.

10.1	Cross stone wall.
10.3	Emerge onto open field and turn left. In another 300 feet, cross row of trees, then turn right, following edge of field uphill, with corn field on left.
10.5	At top of hill, turn left, and follow edge of field. In another 200 feet, turn right, pass through opening in barbed-wire fence, and descend through overgrown field.
10.6	Cross paved Oil City Road (different road from the previous road with same name), and enter field, following stone wall to left, then turn right, and follow posts diagonally across field.
10.8	At end of field, descend, and cross through hollow, then bear left, and ascend from hollow.
10.9	At top of ascent, bear left, and continue along left edge of field for 200 feet to end of field, then bear left, and descend.
11.1	Follow puncheons through swampy thickets, cross bridge over brook, and reach N.J. 284 (end of section). To continue, cross road, and follow Trail uphill into woods (see New Jersey Section Three).

Trail Description, South to North

Miles   **Data**

0.0	From N.J. 284, cross bridge over brook, and follow puncheons through swampy thickets. Cross over stone wall, and bear right, climbing small knoll.
0.2	Reach top of knoll. Continue along right side of field for 200 feet, then turn right, and descend. Cross through hollow, and ascend.
0.3	Reach open field. Follow posts diagonally across field, then turn left at stone wall (edge of woods), and follow along edge of field.
0.5	Reach paved Oil City Road. Cross road, and ascend gradually through overgrown field.
0.6	Pass through opening in barbed-wire fence, and turn

left, following edge of field uphill, with corn field to right. In 200 feet, reach top of hill, and turn right, following edge of field.

0.8   Turn left, and cross row of trees. In another 300 feet, turn right, and reenter woods.

1.0   Cross stone wall.

1.1   Cross bridge over small stream. In another 75 feet, turn left onto paved road, property of Carnegie Industries.

1.3   Turn right onto State Line Road.

1.5   Cross bridge over Wallkill River. Name of road changes to Oil City Road.

1.8   Turn right onto driveway leading into Liberty Sod Farms. Continue straight ahead on dirt road, with sod farm to left.

2.5   Sod farm road makes left turn. Continue on road along south side of sod farm.

2.7   Road makes jog to right, then to left, and continues on dike across sod farm.

3.0   At end of sod farm, turn left, and follow dirt road (abandoned railroad right-of-way) along east side of sod farm.

3.3   Turn right, descend wooden steps, and follow puncheons for about 0.4 mile across wet area.

3.8   Reach paved Wallkill Road (also known as Liberty Corners Road). Turn right, and follow road for 120 feet, then cross road, and follow posts uphill across overgrown field.

3.9   Cross row of trees and stone wall, continue across second field, then reenter woods, and begin to ascend on switchbacks.

4.5   Reach summit of western ridge of Pochuck Mountain, and begin to descend.

4.8   Turn left onto woods road for 30 feet, then turn right, and resume ascent. In about 500 feet, begin steeper ascent on rocky trail.

5.0   Reach crest of middle ridge of Pochuck Mountain, and bear right, following ridge.

5.1   Reach beautiful overlook, with views west across Wallkill Valley to High Point and the Kittatinnies. Begin gradual descent.

5.4   Turn left onto old woods road. Follow road for 150 feet, then bear right onto trail as road turns left.

5.5   Turn left on relocated Trail as old Trail route continues straight ahead, and pass through hemlock grove.

5.6   Cross swampy area on puncheons, and begin to ascend. In another 250 feet, cross dirt private road, and continue to ascend.

5.8   Reach summit of Pochuck Mountain. Side trail to left leads 40 feet to viewpoint over western ridge of mountain. Begin to descend.

6.1   Cross swampy area on puncheons, and continue descent.

6.4   Cross private dirt road.

6.6   Cross stream on rocks, then cross swampy area on puncheons. In another 150 feet, emerge onto open field. Continue along left side of field, with tree line to right.

6.7   Turn right and cross field, then bear left, descending through old field now overgrown with red cedars. Continue steady descent.

6.9   Pass through gap in stone wall, climb steps, and cross wooden bridge over stream, then follow posts across field.

7.0   Reach paved County 565. Cross road, continue across field, then enter woods, and ascend to shoulder of hill.

7.1   Begin to descend, crossing several stone walls.

7.4   Trail runs parallel to stone wall on left, then turns away from stone wall, and ascends briefly.

7.6   Begin steady ascent.

7.7   Cross old woods road, and continue to ascend.

7.8   Trail levels off.

8.0   Bear right, and begin steady descent.

8.1   Cross stone wall, and pass through stand of red cedars. In another 150 feet, reach viewpoint to east over Wawayanda Mountain. Continue to descend.

8.4   At base of descent, emerge onto open fields. Continue across fields, following posts, cross wet area on puncheons, and ascend slightly over rise.

8.5   Reach top of rise, and begin to descend.

8.6   Cross wet area on puncheons, cross stile over stone

wall, and reach paved County 517. Turn right, and follow road.

9.4   Turn left onto Maple Grange Road.

10.0   Cross one-lane bridge over stream.

10.4   Cross bridge over stream.

10.8   Cross railroad tracks.

11.1   Reach N.J. 94 (end of section). To continue on Trail, cross road, and follow hedgerow across fields (see New Jersey Section One).

N.J. 284 (Unionville, New York) to N.J. 23 (High Point)
New Jersey Section Three
9.9 Miles

Brief Description of Section

This section of the Trail completes the crossing of the Kittatinny Valley traveling south along the Trail. It continues to parallel the New York-New Jersey state line while heading in a northwesterly direction. From N.J. 284, the Trail passes through rolling farmlands, pastures, fields, and open woods before climbing to the eastern face of the Kittatinny Ridge. It is pleasant and easy walking. The southern portion of this section is in High Point State Park and passes just below High Point Monument, which marks the highest elevation in New Jersey (1,803 feet). A blue-blazed side trail (0.3 mile round trip) leads to the monument, but much the same panorama of New Jersey, Pennsylvania, and New York is provided from a wooden observation platform directly on the Trail. The Trail turns southwesterly along the ridge to the southern terminus of the section at High Point State Park headquarters.

This section was the first portion of the A.T. in New Jersey to be relocated within the protected Appalachian Trail corridor acquired by the State of New Jersey. It was opened on October 2, 1982, in a ceremony attended by the governor, at which time a cooperative agreement between the NY-NJ TC and the State of New Jersey for the maintenance of the Trail was signed.

Road Approaches

Both the northern and southern ends of this section are accessible by vehicle. At the northern end, the Trail crosses N.J. 284, 0.9 mile south of the center of Unionville, N.Y. Parking for four or five cars is available in a dirt turnout just north of the Trail crossing. At the southern end, the Trail crosses N.J. 23 at the southern driveway of High Point State Park headquarters. A parking lot specifically for A.T. hikers is located just south of park headquarters. The Trail in this section also crosses numerous secondary roads and lanes, but parking along these roads is not recommended.

Public Transportation

Bus service to New York City, operated by Short Line, (212) 736-4700, is available at Port Jervis, New York, about 7.0 miles northwest of the Trail crossing of N.J. 23 (follow N.J. 23 north to junction with U.S. 6; continue west on U.S. 6). Rail service to New York City (via Hoboken), operated by the Metro-North Commuter Railroad, (212) 532-4900, is also available except on Sundays. Public transportation is not available at the northern end of the section.

Maps

For route navigation, refer to Maps Four and Five with this guide. For area detail, refer to the following USGS 7 1/2-minute topographic quadrangles: Unionville, New York-New Jersey; Port Jervis South, New Jersey-New York-Pennsylvania.

Shelters and Campsites

This section has one shelter.
High Point Shelter. Built in 1934; stone shelter with wood floor; 1.7 miles from southern end of section; 0.1 mile from A.T. on blue-blazed side trail; accommodates 8; water from streams near shelter.

Supplies and Services

At the northern end of the section, groceries, sandwiches, and a post office (ZIP Code 10988) are available in Unionville, New York, on N.Y. 284, 0.9 mile north of the Trail crossing. Unionville may also be reached via Lott Road (also known as Jersey Avenue), which crosses the Trail 1.0 mile from the northern end of the section (follow Lott Road to the north for 0.3 mile, then turn left along N.Y. 284 for 0.1 mile).

The southern end has supermarkets and a laundromat on N.J. 23, 4.3 miles northwest of the Trail crossing. Groceries are also available in Colesville, 2.5 miles southeast of the Trail crossing on N.J. 23. Supermarkets, restaurants, and a post office (ZIP Code 12771) are located in Port Jervis, New York, about 7.0 miles northwest of the Trail crossing of N.J. 23 (follow N.J. 23 north to junction with U.S. 6; continue west on U.S. 6). The headquarters of High Point State Park, at the southern end of the section, will accept and hold packages for hikers if marked "hold for arrival" with the name of the hiker and the approximate date of arrival specified (address: High Point State Park, Sussex, N.J. 07461).

Public Accommodations

At the southern end of the section, motels are located on N.J. 23 both 1.4 miles south and 4.4 miles north of the Trail crossing. No accommodations are available at the northern end of the section.

Trail Description, North to South

Miles	Data
0.0	From N.J. 284, enter woods, and ascend for 250 feet to field. Turn right, and skirt field, keeping tree line on right, and turn left up slope of field.
0.3	At end of field, ascend to abandoned railroad grade. Turn right, and follow railroad grade.
0.8	Bear left, leaving railroad grade, and follow stone wall paralleling railroad grade below. After 350 feet, turn left, and continue into woods, crossing two stone walls.
1.0	Pass pond to right of Trail, and reach paved Lott Road (also known as Jersey Avenue). Unionville, New York, is 0.4 mile to right along Lott Road, then left on N.Y. 284. Turn right, cross bridge over stream, and continue along road for 175 feet, then turn left, and ascend into woods, passing house to right of Trail.
1.1	Enter open field, and bear right across field.
1.2	Reenter woods, and ascend gradually, crossing numerous old quarry roads.

1.5   Reach crest of hill, and begin to descend, following left fork of trail.

1.7   Reach paved Quarry Road. Cross road, and reenter woods, passing old quarry pit and house on right.

2.0   Reach paved Unionville Road (County 651). Cross road diagonally to left, and reenter woods.

2.1   Cross stone wall, and emerge onto open field. Continue straight ahead, ascending hill. Cross farm road, and continue ahead on old farm road. In 150 feet, turn left, and pass through fieldbreak. Continue through another fieldbreak, then pass through abandoned apple orchard.

2.4   Reach dirt Goldsmith Lane. Cross road, and enter overgrown successional field. In 300 feet, bear right, and cross stone wall.

2.5   Follow puncheons across Vernie Swamp for next 0.3 mile.

2.8   Cross bridge over stream. In another 100 feet, cross gravel Goldsmith Road, then climb through field, keeping trees and low stone wall (New York-New Jersey boundary) to right.

3.0   Reach crest of field, with excellent view of High Point Monument directly ahead. To rear, Pochuck Mountain is on the horizon. Descend, with pines on right.

3.1   Pass pond to left, crossing concrete dam (outlet of pond). Emerge onto field. Cross field, bearing left, and reenter woods. Continue over gentle hill.

3.2   Reach crest of hill, and descend.

3.3   Reach paved Goodrich Road. Cross road, pass briefly through woods, and enter overgrown field.

3.4   Cross small stream.

3.6   Bear left, then turn right, and cross log bridge over stream. In another 200 feet, cross bridge over second stream, then turn left, and ascend.

3.9   Reach crest of rise, and begin to descend.

4.0   Pass through very muddy area. Cross stream, and bear right.

4.1   Follow stone wall to left for 200 feet. Reach intersection of stone walls, with fence on right wall. Turn right, and,

	in 60 feet, come out on successional field with cedars. Continue through field, bearing right.
4.2	Turn right, and cross brook, then follow posts across overgrown field.
4.3	Reach paved Gemmer Road. Turn right, and follow road for 200 feet, then turn left, and reenter woods, passing through swampy area.
4.4	Turn left, and cross small brook. Bear right, and ascend, passing through swampy area.
4.5	Emerge onto abandoned field, and follow posts diagonally to left across field.
4.6	Cross stone wall, and reenter woods.
4.9	Reach Ferguson Road, passable by car. Turn right, and follow road for 120 feet, then turn left, cross stile, and enter pasture. Follow blazes across pasture.
5.0	Cross boggy area on puncheons, then cross bridge over stream. Bear left, and follow posts across pasture, crossing muddy area.
5.1	At intersection of stone walls, bear right, and cross over stile into cultivated field. (This section of Trail corridor is being farmed under lease arrangement with former owner, whose family has worked the land for five generations.) Skirt field, following tree line on left.
5.2	At end of field, turn right, continuing to follow tree line on left, then cross overgrown stone wall, and turn left. Again skirt field, following tree line on left.
5.4	At end of field, turn right, continuing to follow tree line on left, then turn left, passing pond on right. Cross over stile, and turn right, skirting field. In another 300 feet, turn right, and pass through electrified gate at farm maintenance road. *Use care and close gate.* Turn left, and ascend along left side of pasture.
5.6	Cross barbed-wire fence near crest of pasture, and descend along left side of cultivated fields.
5.7	Pass through stile, and reenter woods.
5.9	Follow blazes carefully across and along many old stone walls.
6.1	Reach dirt-and-gravel Courtright Road, passable by

	car. Cross road, and continue straight ahead through woods.
6.2	Cross stream.
6.3	Cross grassy woods road, then cross stream, and emerge onto overgrown field. Continue across field.
6.4	Reenter woods, and cross swampy area, then cross several stone walls.
6.8	Leave woods, and pass through fields, skirting to right of trees on rise.
6.9	Reach paved County 519. Cross road, bearing slightly to left, and reenter woods, ascending on switchbacks.
7.1	After passing through swampy area, emerge onto overgrown clearing. In 175 feet, turn left onto dirt road, and follow road for 150 feet, then turn right, and pass through pasture.
7.2	Turn right, and ascend, with views to right, then make sharp left turn, and continue to ascend.
7.4	Trail bears left and levels off, passing through gaps in several stone walls.
8.0	Cross intermittent brook at head of ravine, then bear left, and pass over stone wall. In another 150 feet, Trail turns right at intersection. Former Trail route descends along ravine. *Do not descend.*
8.2	Turn right, and ascend. Blue-blazed side trail continues straight ahead 0.1 mile to **High Point Shelter**. Water is available from streams before and beyond shelter.
8.7	Turn left at intersection with blue-blazed side trail which leads north to High Point Monument, marking the highest elevation in New Jersey (1,803 feet).
8.9	Reach wooden observation platform. Excellent 360-degree view. Kittatinny Valley lies to the east, with Pochuck Mountain in the distance and Wawayanda Mountain on the horizon. New York City skyline may be seen looking to the southeast. To the southwest is Delaware Water Gap. In foreground to the west are Lake Marcia and High Point Lodge, with the Pocono Mountains of Pennsylvania in the distance. Northwest lies Catskill Plateau. High Point Monument dominates ridge

to the north. Continue south along ridge, passing through scrub oak and blueberry bushes.

9.0   Bear right, and continue along ridge, as former Trail route (now abandoned) descends from ridge.

9.1   Turn left and descend, as former Trail route (now abandoned) continues straight ahead. In another 200 feet, descend steeply, then continue descending more moderately.

9.8   Leave woods, and cross lawn.

9.9   Reach paved N.J. 23 (end of section). To continue, cross road at south driveway of High Point State Park headquarters, and reenter woods at south end of parking lot (see New Jersey Section Four). Water is available at headquarters. Please sign trail register at office desk.

Trail Description, South to North

Miles   **Data**

0.0   From N.J. 23, bear northeast across lawn for 300 feet and enter woods. Gradually ascend through scrub oak and blueberry bushes while bearing left, and reach shoulder of ridge.

0.8   Ascend steeply for 180 feet. In another 200 feet, former Trail route enters from left. High Point Monument is visible directly ahead. Trail turns right.

0.9   Bear left, and continue along ridge, as former Trail route (now abandoned) descends from ridge.

1.0   Reach wooden observation platform. Excellent 360-degree view. Kittatinny Valley, through which Trail passes, lies to the east, with Pochuck Mountain in distance and Wawayanda Mountain on the horizon. New York City skyline may be seen looking southeast. To the southwest is Delaware Water Gap. In foreground to the west are Lake Marcia and High Point Lodge, with Pocono Mountains of Pennsylvania in the distance. Northwest lies Catskill Plateau. Continue along ridge, and descend into saddle below monument.

1.2   Trail turns right and begins descent off ridge. Blue-blazed side trail continues along ridge to High Point Monument, which marks highest elevation in New Jersey (1,803 feet).

1.7   Blue-blazed side trail leads right 0.1 mile to **High Point Shelter**. Water is available from streams before and beyond shelter. A.T. turns left.

1.9   Turn left. Abandoned Trail route enters from right. Pass over stone wall, cross intermittent brook at head of ravine, and continue along ridge, passing through gaps in several stone walls.

2.5   Trail bears right, descending off ridge.

2.6   Turn sharp right, and continue to descend, with views to left.

2.7   Turn left, and leave woods. Pass through field, and, in 240 feet, turn left on dirt road. Follow dirt road for 150 feet, then turn right. Pass through overgrown clearing, and reenter woods, passing through swampy area.

3.0   Descend on switchbacks, and reach paved County 519. Cross road, bearing slightly to left, and pass through fields, skirting to left of trees on rise.

3.1   Reenter woods, and cross several stone walls.

3.5   Cross swampy area, and emerge onto overgrown field. Continue across field.

3.6   Reenter woods, and cross stream, then cross grassy woods road. In another 350 feet, cross second stream.

3.8   Reach dirt-and-gravel Courtwright Road, passable by car. Cross road, and follow blazes carefully along and through many old stone walls.

4.2   Pass through stile, and enter cultivated fields. Skirt fields to right, following stone wall.

4.3   Cross barbed-wire fence near crest of field, and descend along right side of pasture.

4.4   Near end of field, turn right, and pass through electrified wire gate at farm maintenance road. *Use care and close gate.* (This section of Trail corridor is being farmed under lease arrangement with former owner.) Skirt left side of field for 300 feet, then turn left, and pass through stile. Pass pond on left.

4.5   At end of pond, bear right, and skirt edge of field. Turn left, and continue along right side of field.

4.6   Turn right, crossing overgrown stone wall, and enter lower field. Again skirt field by keeping tree line on right.

4.8   At intersection of stone walls, cross stile into lower pasture. Bear left, and follow posts across pasture, crossing muddy area. Cross bridge over stream, and walk on puncheons through boggy area. Continue across pasture to road.

5.0   Cross stile, and reach Ferguson Road, passable by car. Turn right, and follow road for 120 feet, then turn left, and reenter woods.

5.3   Cross stone wall, and emerge onto abandoned field. Continue diagonally to right, following posts through field. Reenter woods, descending gradually, and pass through swampy area.

5.5   Cross small brook, and turn right, passing through swampy area.

5.6   Reach paved Gemmer Road. Turn right, and follow road for 200 feet, then turn left into overgrown field, and follow posts across field.

5.7   Cross brook, and turn left. Continue through successional field with cedars, while bearing right.

5.8   Reenter woods. In another 60 feet, reach intersection of stone walls, with fence on right wall. Turn left, and continue with wall on right for 200 feet, then bear left, turning away from wall.

5.9   Cross stream, and bear right, passing through very muddy area.

6.0   Reach crest of rise, and descend gradually, with stream below on right.

6.3   Cross log bridge over stream, and turn left. In another 200 feet, cross bridge over second stream, and bear left. Pass through overgrown field.

6.5   Cross small stream. In another 300 feet, reenter woods.

6.6   Reach paved Goodrich Road. Cross road, and continue up small hill.

6.7   Reach crest of hill, and descend. In 225 feet, cross field.

6.8   With pond on right, reenter woods. In 125 feet, cross concrete dam (outlet of pond). Bear right through pines, then ascend hill, keeping pines on left.

6.9   Reach crest of field, with good view of Pochuck Mountain in the distance. To rear (west) is excellent view of High Point Monument. Trail descends, with trees and low stone wall (New York-New Jersey boundary) on left.

7.1   Cross gravel Goldsmith Road. In another 100 feet, cross bridge over stream, then follow puncheons across Vernie Swamp for next 0.3 mile.

7.4   Cross stone wall, and ascend gradually through overgrown successional field.

7.5   Reach dirt Goldsmith Lane. Cross road, and pass through overgrown apple orchard. Cross overgrown fields, passing through several fieldbreaks.

7.7   Turn right onto old farm road. In 150 feet, reach intersecting farm road. Continue straight ahead down hill, then cross stone wall, and reenter woods.

7.9   Reach paved Unionville Road (County 651). Unionville, New York, is 1.2 miles to left. Cross road diagonally to left, and reenter woods, passing house on left and open quarry pit below.

8.2   Reach paved Quarry Road. Cross road, and ascend hill.

8.4   Reach crest of hill, and begin to descend. Follow Trail carefully, crossing numerous old quarry roads.

8.7   Emerge onto open field. Follow Trail across field.

8.8   Turn left, and reenter woods. In 125 feet, pass house on left as Trail bears left.

8.9   Reach paved Lott Road (also known as Jersey Avenue). Unionville, New York, is 0.4 mile to left along Lott Road, then left again at N.Y. 284. Turn right, and follow road for 175 feet, crossing bridge over stream, then turn left at end of bridge, and reenter woods. Follow shore of pond for 100 feet, then turn right, and continue into woods.

9.1   Turn right, and follow old stone wall on left for 350 feet, then turn left, and descend to abandoned railroad grade. Turn right, and follow railroad grade.

9.6   Turn left, leaving railroad grade, and descend to field. Skirt field, following tree line to left.

9.9   Turn left, reentering woods, and descend to paved N.J. 284 (end of section). To continue, cross road, and follow Trail straight ahead (see New Jersey Section Two).

N.J. 23 (High Point) to U.S. 206 (Culvers Gap)
New Jersey Section Four
14.3 Miles

Brief Description of Section

The Trail in this section runs along the ridge of the Kittatinny Mountains through High Point State Park and Stokes State Forest. The Trail follows a rocky footpath through hickory and scrub-oak forests, with some hemlocks and pitch pines. There are many good viewpoints on both sides of the ridge. The elevation at N.J. 23 is about 1,500 feet, and, at U.S. 206, it is 935 feet. The highest point in this section is 1,653 feet, at Sunrise Mountain.

Many side trails intersect the A.T. in this section. Descriptions of these trails may be found in the *New York Walk Book*, published by the New York-New Jersey Trail Conference and also available through ATC, and in brochures available at the headquarters of High Point State Park and Stokes State Forest. (Office of High Point is at the northern end of the section; office of Stokes is about 0.5 mile northwest of the southern end of the section along U.S. 206.) These trails are also shown on Maps 17 and 18 of the Kittatinny Trails map set published by the New York-New Jersey Trail Conference.

Road Approaches

Both the northern and southern ends of this section are accessible by vehicle. At the northern end, the Trail crosses N.J. 23 at the southern driveway of High Point State Park headquarters. A parking lot specifically for A.T. hikers is located just south of park headquarters. At the southern end, the Trail crosses U.S. 206 in Culvers Gap, 3.4 miles northwest of Branchville. A parking area is adjacent to the A.T., 0.3 mile north of the Trail crossing of U.S. 206, on Sunrise Mountain Road just north of its intersection with Upper North Shore Road.

Road access is also available at Deckertown Turnpike, also known as Mashipacong Road, which crosses the Trail 5.2 miles from the northern end of the section. In addition, road access is available via Sunrise Mountain Road, which leads to a parking area on Sunrise Mountain, 5.5 miles (along the A.T.) from the southern end of the section. (From U.S. 206, proceed north on Upper North Shore Road for 0.3 mile, then turn left on Sunrise Mountain Road, and continue for 4.8 miles to parking area at end of road.)

Public Transportation

Bus service to New York City, operated by Short Line, (212) 736-4700, is available at Port Jervis, New York, about 7.0 miles northwest of the Trail crossing of N.J. 23 (follow N.J. 23 north to junction with U.S. 6; continue west on U.S. 6). Rail service to New York City (via Hoboken), operated by the Metro-North Commuter Railroad, (212) 532-4900, is also available except on Sundays. No public transportation is available at the southern end of the section.

Maps

For route navigation, refer to Map Five with this guide. For area detail, refer to the following USGS 7 1/2-minute topographic quadrangles: Port Jervis South, New Jersey-New York-Pennsylvania; Branchville, New Jersey; Culvers Gap, New Jersey-Pennsylvania. Other references are NY-NJ TC Trail Maps Nos. 17 and 18 (Kittatinny Trails-North).

Shelters and Campsites

This section has three shelters.

Rutherford Shelter. Built in 1967 by State of New Jersey; log shelter with dirt floor; 2.5 miles from northern end of section; 0.4 mile from A.T. on blue-blazed side trail; accommodates 6; water from nearby spring.

Mashipacong Shelter. Built in 1936; stone shelter with wood floor; 5.4 miles from northern end of section; 8.6 miles from southern end of section; accommodates 8; water from pump at Trail crossing of Deckertown Turnpike (Mashipacong Road), 0.2 mile to the north along Trail.

Gren Anderson Shelter. Built in1958 by New York Section of Green Mountain Club, of which Anderson was a member; log shelter with wood floor; 3.1 miles from southern end of section; 0.3 mile from A.T. on blue-blazed side trail; accommodates 8; water from spring on side trail 200 feet beyond shelter.

Supplies and Services

The northern end of the section has supermarkets and a laundromat on N.J. 23, 4.3 miles northwest of the Trail crossing. Groceries are also available in Colesville, 2.5 miles southeast of the Trail crossing on N.J. 23. Supermarkets, restaurants, and a post office (ZIP Code 12771) are located in Port Jervis, New York, about 7.0 miles northwest of the Trail crossing of N.J. 23 (follow N.J. 23 north to junction with U.S. 6; continue west on U.S. 6). The headquarters of High Point State Park, at the northern end of the section, will accept and hold packages for hikers if marked "hold for arrival," with the name of the hiker and the approximate date of arrival specified (address: High Point State Park, Sussex, N.J. 07461).

At the southern end of the section, a limited selection of groceries may be obtained at Worthington's Bakery, immediately to the west of the Trail crossing of U.S. 206. A grocery store is located on U.S. 206, 1.6 miles southeast of the Trail crossing. Meals are available at a restaurant 0.1 mile west of the Trail crossing. The Stokes Forest Sport Shop, which sells freeze-dried foods and some camping equipment, is 0.2 mile west. Branchville has a post office (ZIP Code 07826) and a laundromat, 3.4 miles southeast of the Trail crossing of U.S. 206.

Public Accommodations

At the northern end of the section, motels are located on N.J. 23, both 1.4 miles south and 4.4 miles north of the Trail crossing. At the southern end, motels are located on U.S. 206, both 2.5 miles east and 1.9 miles west of the Trail crossing.

Trail Description, North to South

Miles	Data

0.0   From N.J. 23, turn into exit of driveway of parking lot at headquarters of High Point State Park. Please sign register at park headquarters. Reenter woods at south end of parking lot and, in 250 feet, pass unmarked trail to left leading to day-use parking area.

0.2   Cross red-blazed Iris Trail, marked by white post to left of A.T. Ascend slightly.

0.3   Turn left onto old woods road.

0.4   Turn right, leaving road, and ascend to ridge.

0.6   Reach crest of ridge, and turn left.

0.9   To right, Blue Dot Trail descends to Sawmill Lake.

1.0   Reach viewpoint to west over Sawmill Lake. Descend to left into interior valley.

1.3   Reach valley floor, and ascend steeply to eastern ridge.

1.4   Reach top of eastern ridge at viewpoint back over the valley. Pocono Mountains are visible in the distance to left. Trail crosses to opposite side of ridge.

1.5   Reach first of a series of viewpoints to east. Below is Lake Rutherford, water supply for town of Sussex. Trail continues along ridge.

1.8   After descent, turn right.

2.3   Reach beautiful viewpoint from open rocks.

2.5   Reach Dutch Shoe Rock, with views to the northeast. Blue-blazed trail to left descends 0.4 mile to **Rutherford Shelter** and nearby spring. Continue across large open rocks, then reenter woods and begin descent.

3.0   Cross stream, and ascend.

3.3   Turn right onto red-blazed Iris Trail (woods road). (To left, Iris Trail can be used as alternate route back to N.J. 23.) In 300 feet, turn sharp left, leaving Iris Trail, and descend steeply into swampy area.

3.5   Ascend slightly, then descend into another swampy area.

3.7   Cross stream, and ascend gradually.

3.8   Turn left, and ascend steeply over rocks, then turn right, and continue gradual ascent.

4.2   Cross cleared strip of land (buried pipeline). Short trail to left leads to viewpoint to east over farm landscape. In 140 feet, Trail forks to right, away from old road (which continues onto private land).

4.4   Pass private home on left.

4.6   Cross red-blazed Iris Trail again. (To right, this trail can be used as an alternate route back to N.J. 23.) A.T. begins to descend.

4.7   Cross swampy area on logs.

5.0   Pass through swampy area, then ascend gradually.

5.3   Reach parking area and pump for water, then cross Deckertown Turnpike (Mashipacong Road) diagonally to the left, and continue to ascend.

5.5   Reach **Mashipacong Shelter**. Trail reenters woods at far right edge of clearing.

6.2   Turn left onto old woods road (Swenson Road). Follow road for 225 feet, then turn right as road curves to left, and ascend on footpath.

6.7   Reach top of rise and begin to descend, passing through mountain-laurel thicket.

7.0   At base of descent, turn right.

7.1   Cross outlet of swamp to left of Trail. In 250 feet, cross stone wall, and begin to ascend rather steeply through white birches.

7.3   Reach top of hill, and begin to descend.

7.4   Cross stone wall, and continue descent.

7.6   Reach rocky area, and begin to ascend.

7.8   Reach top of knoll, and begin to descend.

8.0   Cross dirt Crigger Road, and ascend.

8.7   Pass parking area for Sunrise Mountain to right of Trail. Restrooms are here. In 300 feet, path from parking area joins A.T., which continues ascent on wide footpath.

8.9   Reach shelter at summit of Sunrise Mountain (1,653 feet), with good views east and west. Shelter has a roof but no walls and provides protection from rain, except in high winds. No camping permitted at shelter. From southeast corner of shelter, descend for 150 feet, then come out on open ledges, with beautiful views to east. At southeast corner of clearing, reenter woods, and descend, turning right along rocks.

9.0 Pass viewpoint through trees to left, as Trail briefly levels off, then continues gradual descent.

9.4 Ascend over knoll, then descend gradually.

9.8 Reach yellow-blazed Tinsley Trail, which descends to right, crossing Sunrise Mountain Road in 60 yards and continuing to overnight camping area at Lake Ocquittunk. A.T. ascends briefly and continues along west edge of ridge, with views to west through trees.

10.4 Ascend, then descend gradually.

10.8 For next 0.1 mile, pass several ponds or swamps (in wet season) to left of Trail.

11.1 Pass through several short, wet sections.

11.2 Reach blue-blazed Stony Brook Trail, which leads to right, reaching **Gren Anderson Shelter** in 0.3 mile and spring 200 feet beyond shelter.

11.4 Cross Stony Brook.

12.2 At viewpoint to west in pines, reach green-blazed Tower Trail, which descends to right.

12.3 After brief ascent, reach Culver Fire Tower, which provides 360-degree view. Lake Owassa is visible to southwest, just left of Kittatinny Ridge, and Lake Kittatinny is visible to right of ridge. Culver Lake is hidden behind the ridge. A.T. continues on footpath at southeast corner of clearing. In 100 feet, it turns right on a level, gravel road, and passes trail register (please sign). (To left, gravel road descends to east over private land.)

12.4 Road ends at radio transmitter and adjacent cinderblock building. Trail enters woods to right and begins to descend, with Culver Lake soon visible through trees to left.

12.8 Cross small grassy clearing.

13.3 Reach viewpoint over Culver Lake, with view somewhat obscured by trees.

13.4 Turn sharp right. In 200 feet, reach viewpoint to west over Kittatinny Lake. Trail again turns right and continues to descend.

13.5	Turn sharp left, and continue to descend.
13.8	Reach paved Sunrise Mountain Road. Turn left, and follow road.
13.9	Pass exit from parking area to right.
14.0	After passing entrance to parking area, turn right on Upper North Shore Road.
14.3	Reach U.S. 206 (end of section). To continue, turn left, and follow U.S. 206 for 0.1 mile, then cross U.S. 206, and enter woods (see New Jersey Section Five).

Trail Description, South to North

Miles   **Data**

0.0	From intersection of U.S. 206 and Upper North Shore Road, proceed north on Upper North Shore Road.
0.3	Turn left onto Sunrise Mountain Road, and pass entrance to parking area on left.
0.4	Pass exit from parking area on left.
0.5	Turn right, and enter woods, ascending gradually.
0.8	Turn right, and ascend more steeply.
0.9	Turn left at viewpoint over Kittatinny Lake. In 200 feet, turn left again, and continue to ascend, with views of Culver Lake through the trees on the right.
1.0	Reach viewpoint over Culver Lake, with view somewhat obscured by trees.
1.5	Cross small, grassy clearing.
1.9	Pass radio transmitter and adjacent cinder-block building. Continue on grassy dirt road that soon becomes gravel.
2.0	Pass trail register (please sign) and turn left from gravel road (which descends to east over private land) onto footpath. In 100 feet, reach Culver Fire Tower, which provides 360-degree view. Lake Owassa is visible to southwest, just left of Kittatinny Ridge, and Lake Kittatinny is visible to right of ridge. Culver Lake is hidden behind ridge. A.T. continues at northwest corner of clearing by a rocky ledge, where it turns right and begins to descend.

2.1   At viewpoint to west in pines, reach green-blazed Tower Trail, which descends to left.

2.3   Bear left at fork in Trail.

2.9   Cross Stony Brook.

3.1   Reach blue-blazed Stony Brook Trail, which leads to left, reaching **Gren Anderson Shelter** in 0.3 mile and spring 200 feet beyond shelter.

3.2   Bear left at fork in Trail, and pass through several short, wet sections.

3.4   For next 0.1 mile, pass several ponds or swamps (in wet season) on right side of Trail.

3.8   Ascend gradually, then descend, coming out on west side of ridge, with views to west through trees.

4.5   After short, steep descent, reach yellow-blazed Tinsley Trail, which descends to left, crossing Sunrise Mountain Road in 60 yards and continuing to overnight camping area at Lake Ocquittunk.

4.6   Ascend over knoll, then descend.

5.0   Begin gradual ascent of Sunrise Mountain.

5.3   Reach viewpoint through trees to right as Trail levels off.

5.4   After short climb, come out on open ledges, with beautiful views to east. Continue climbing for 150 feet, and reach stone shelter at summit of Sunrise Mountain (1,653 feet), with good views east and west. Shelter has a roof but no walls and provides protection from rain, except in high winds. No camping permitted at shelter. Trail continues on wide footpath from northeast corner of shelter.

5.6   Descend stone steps, then take right fork as wide footpath to left continues to parking area and restrooms. A.T. begins to descend.

6.3   Cross dirt Crigger Road. After short descent, begin to ascend.

6.5   Reach top of knoll, and begin to descend.

6.7   Reach rocky area, and begin to ascend.

6.9   Cross stone wall, and continue to ascend.

7.0   Reach top of hill, and descend rather steeply through white birches.

7.1   At base of descent, cross stone wall. In 250 feet, cross outlet of swamp to right of Trail.

7.3   Turn left, and begin to ascend, soon passing through mountain-laurel thicket.

7.6   Reach top of rise, and begin gradual descent.

8.1   Turn left onto old woods road (Swenson Road). Follow road for 225 feet, then turn right, and reenter woods on footpath.

8.8   Reach **Mashipacong Shelter**. Turn left and descend steadily.

9.0   Cross paved Deckertown Turnpike (Mashipacong Road) diagonally to the left, and reach parking area and pump for water. Continue to descend.

9.3   Pass through swampy area, and soon begin to ascend.

9.6   Cross swampy area on logs.

9.7   Cross red-blazed Iris Trail. A.T. levels off and continues along ridge, with limited views through trees to right.

9.9   Pass private home on right.

10.1   Turn left onto woods road. In 140 feet, cross cleared strip of land (buried pipeline). Short trail to right leads to viewpoint to east over farm landscape. Continue along ridge.

10.4   Begin gradual descent.

10.5   Make sharp left turn, and descend steeply over rocks, then turn right, and continue gradual descent.

10.6   Cross stream, and begin gradual ascent.

10.7   Pass small swampy area to left of Trail.

10.8   Make short descent, then continue to ascend.

10.9   After passing through swampy area, begin steep ascent.

11.0   At top of steep ascent, turn right onto red-blazed Iris Trail (woods road). In another 300 feet, turn left, leaving Iris Trail, and ascend briefly, then turn right and continue along ridge.

11.2   Turn left and begin to descend.

11.3   Cross stream.

11.5   Begin steady ascent.

11.8   After crossing large open rocks, reach Dutch Shoe Rock, with views to the northeast of Lake Rutherford, the water supply for the town of Sussex. Blue-blazed trail to right descends 0.3 mile to **Rutherford Shelter** and nearby spring. A.T. continues along ridge.

12.0   Reach beautiful viewpoint from open rocks. Trail continues along ridge, with some limited views through trees to right.

12.5   Turn left, and ascend.

12.8   Reach viewpoint from open rocks, with Lake Rutherford visible to the southeast. Trail turns left and crosses to opposite side of ridge.

12.9   Reach viewpoint to left over interior valley, with Pocono Mountains visible in the distance to the left. Turn left, and descend steeply into the valley.

13.0   Reach floor of valley, and begin ascent to western ridge.

13.3   Reach viewpoint to west over Sawmill Lake. Turn right, and follow ridge.

13.4   To left, Blue Dot Trail descends to Sawmill Lake.

13.7   Turn right, away from ridge, and soon descend steeply.

13.9   Turn left onto old woods road.

14.0   Turn right, leaving road, and descend slightly.

14.1   Cross red-blazed Iris Trail, marked by white post to right of A.T.

14.3   Pass unmarked trail to right leading to day-use parking area. In 250 feet, turn right, follow exit driveway of headquarters of High Point State Park (please sign trail register at park headquarters), and reach N.J. 23 (end of section). To continue, cross N.J. 23 and follow posts across lawn, then enter woods (see New Jersey Section Three).

U.S. 206 (Culvers Gap) to Millbrook-Blairstown Road
New Jersey Section Five
14.6 Miles

Brief Description of Section

This section follows the ridge of the Kittatinny Mountains. The route is mostly wooded, with many good views on both sides of the crest. Although rocky in many areas, the Trail is relatively level, especially in the southern part, with some moderate up-and-down stretches and occasional short, steep sections. Elevation at Millbrook-Blairstown Road, the southern point of the section, is 1,260 feet. The high point of the section—on the ridge north of Crater Lake—is 1,606 feet, and the lowest point is 935 feet, at U.S. 206 in Culvers Gap.

The section passes through oak and hickory hardwood forests, with some conifers, such as pitch pine, white pine, red cedar, and hemlock, and rhododendron. Blueberries are plentiful in season.

This section has one important side trail—the one-and-one-half-mile trail to Buttermilk Falls. Although rather steep in parts, the trail leads to a beautiful waterfall and is well worth the effort.

Road Approaches

Both the northern and southern ends of this section are accessible by vehicle. At the northern end, the Trail crosses U.S. 206 in Culvers Gap, 3.4 miles northwest of Branchville. A parking area is located adjacent to the A.T., 0.3 mile north of the Trail crossing of U.S. 206, on Sunrise Mountain Road just north of its intersection with Upper North Shore Road. At the southern end, the Trail crosses Millbrook-Blairstown Road, 6.2 miles northwest of Blairstown and 1.1 miles southeast of Millbrook Village, a collection of historic buildings. Parking is available at the Trail crossing.

The Trail in this section also crosses Flatbrookville Road 3.8 miles from the southern end of the section. Vehicle access is available only from the west. Parking is available both 150 feet east and 150 feet west of the Trail crossing. Access from the west is also available at Brink Road, 4.6 miles from the northern end of the section.

Public Transportation

Public transportation is not available at the northern end of this section. Bus service to New York City, operated by Lakeland Bus Lines, (201) 366-0600, is available in Blairstown, 6.2 miles southeast along Millbrook-Blairstown Road from the southern end.

Maps

For route navigation, refer to Maps Five and Six with this guide. For area detail, refer to the following USGS 7 1/2-minute topographic quadrangles: Culvers Gap, New Jersey-Pennsylvania; Newton West, New Jersey (small corner only); Flatbrookville, New Jersey-Pennsylvania. Other references are NY-NJ TC Trail Maps Nos. 16 and 17 (Kittatinny Trails-North and South).

Shelters and Campsites

This section has one shelter.

Brink Road Shelter. Built in 1970; 3.6 miles from north end of section; 900 feet off Trail on dirt road; accommodates 5; dirt floor; water from spring 350 feet beyond shelter on blue-blazed trail.

In addition, for thru-hikers, camping is permitted along the Trail on the southern 10 miles of this section, from about 1.0 mile south of Brink Road to Millbrook-Blairstown Road, which pass through the Delaware Water Gap National Recreation Area. It is subject to the following conditions: Camping is permitted only in areas that are more than 0.5 mile from road accesses or the boundaries of the national recreation area. No camping is permitted from 0.5 mile south of Flatbrookville Road to 1.0 mile north of Lake Success (Crater Lake), where the Wallpack Township-Stillwater Township boundary crosses the Trail (about 2.5 miles north of Flatbrookville Road).

Where camping is permitted, hikers must camp not more than 100 feet from the Trail and not less than 200 feet from other campsites. Camping is prohibited within 100 feet of any stream, and any one campsite is limited to 10 persons. No open fires are permitted.

Camping is not permitted along the Trail on the northern 4.5 miles of this section, which pass through Stokes State Forest, except at the Brink Road Shelter.

Supplies and Services

At the northern end of the section, a limited selection of groceries may be obtained at Worthington's Bakery, immediately to the west of the Trail crossing of U.S. 206. A grocery store is located on U.S. 206, 1.6 miles southeast of the Trail crossing. Meals are available at a restaurant 0.1 mile west of the Trail crossing. The Stokes Forest Sport Shop, which sells freeze-dried foods and some camping equipment, is 0.2 mile west. A post office and a laundromat are located in Branchville (ZIP Code 07826), 3.4 miles southeast of the Trail crossing on U.S. 206. At the southern end of the section, groceries, meals, a laundromat, and a post office (ZIP Code 07825) are available in Blairstown, 6.2 miles southeast of the Trail crossing of Millbrook-Blairstown Road.

Public Accommodations

At the northern end of the section, motels are located on U.S. 206, both 2.5 miles east and 1.9 miles west of the Trail crossing. At the southern end, motels are located in Blairstown, 6.2 miles to the southeast.

Trail Description, North to South

Miles	Data
0.0	From intersection of U.S. 206 and Upper North Shore Road, proceed east on U.S. 206, passing rest area pull-off on left.
0.1	Turn right, cross road, and enter woods on footpath, ascending gradually.
0.2	Turn left onto old woods road, and continue to ascend.

0.4   Trail levels off.

0.6   Cross gravel road, route of gold, dark-brown-blazed Acropolis Trail, and resume steady ascent.

0.9   Reach clearing at crest of ridge. Trail turns left, with views to left of U.S. 206 below, then enters woods.

1.4   Reach viewpoint in large cleared area. Culver Lake and U.S. 206 are visible looking back to left, and Culver Fire Tower is visible looking to north along Trail.

2.1   After gradual ascent, reach Jacob's Ladder Trail, with blue-gray markings, which descends about 0.3 mile to right to junction of Coss Road and Woods Road. Trail ascends gradually, then levels off, ascends steadily, and descends briefly.

2.5   Unmarked side trail to left leads to overlook of Lake Owassa.

3.1   Pass field of rocks and boulders to left of Trail. Four hundred feet beyond, unmarked side trail to left leads to overlook.

3.3   Begin descent from crest of ridge.

3.7   Reach dirt Brink Road. (Left 0.5 mile to Lake Owassa Road; not passable by car. Right 2.5 miles to Wallpack Center; passable up to 0.2 mile west of Trail crossing.) **Brink Road Shelter** is on right side of road, 900 feet to right of Trail crossing. Blue-blazed trail leads to shelter and to spring 350 feet behind shelter, a dependable water source. Trail crosses road, enters woods to right, and begins to ascend.

4.1   Trail levels off, descends slightly, then resumes ascent.

4.4   Reach cleared area on height of ridge. Sweeping views to right of Wallpack Valley, and views through trees to left.

4.5   Reenter wooded area. Trail begins to descend, passing several rock ledges with views to right.

4.8   Turn left on old dirt road, and begin to ascend.

5.1   Turn left off dirt road, and reach rocky, cleared area, with views through trees to left. Trail begins to descend.

5.6   Cross short swampy area on rocks, and begin gradual ascent of Rattlesnake Mountain.

6.0   Reach rock outcrop marking summit of Rattlesnake Mountain (1,492 feet), with beautiful views to right. Trail begins to descend, passing through burned-out area, with views to right.

6.3   Blue-blazed trail to left leads 200 feet to water source. In another 50 feet on A.T., cross stream. Two hundred feet past stream, Trail turns left and begins to ascend.

6.8   Blue-blazed trail on right leads 75 feet to viewpoint. Trail levels off.

7.4   Reach viewpoint to west from open rocks.

7.6   Turn right onto gravel road. Trail continues along gravel roads for next 1.4 miles, with occasional views of Pocono Mountains to west.

7.8   Blue-blazed trail to right descends for 1.5 miles to Buttermilk Falls, a dependable water source. (See description of trail at end of this section.) In another 125 feet, turn right onto gravel road.

8.7   Turn right onto intersecting gravel road.

9.0   Blue-blazed trail to left leads 150 feet to viewpoint overlooking Crater Lake. Fifty feet beyond this point, Trail leaves gravel road and turns right on footpath. In another 150 feet, reach viewpoint to west. Trail turns left, crosses gravel road, and, in another 150 feet, steeply descends face of escarpment.

9.1   Trail makes right turn. In another 300 feet, cross old gravel road diagonally to right, and reenter woods.

9.4   Pass rock-strewn bog on left.

9.6   Ascend steeply to right of smooth rock.

10.6   Cross dirt road, and turn right on footpath into woods.

10.8   Reach paved Flatbrookville Road. Blue-blazed side trail leads to pump, a tested water source. Trail crosses road, then turns right and follows paved road for 100 feet, where it turns left on dirt road.

11.1   Trail register is located to right of Trail. Please sign. One hundred and twenty five feet beyond this point, road to left leads about 125 feet to viewpoint overlooking northern end of Fairview Lake.

11.5   Clearing to left of Trail provides view of Fairview Lake below.

12.4	Dirt road ends. Trail enters woods to left on footpath.
13.8	Reach clearing for powerline. Sand Pond of Camp No-Be-Bo-Sco, Bergen Council, Boy Scouts of America, is visible below to left. Trail turns right after passing powerline tower and follows powerline across ridge for about 0.1 mile. At other side of ridge are views to west of Wallkill Valley and Pocono Plateau. Trail curves to left and reenters woods.
14.0	Descend steeply, then turn left.
14.2	Turn left, skirting north end of swamp, then turn right on dirt road, cross outlet of swamp, and ascend, with swamp to right of Trail.
14.4	Bear right at fork.
14.5	Reach paved Millbrook-Blairstown Road. Turn left, and follow paved road for 0.1 mile.
14.6	Cross paved road, and turn right on woods road (end of section). To continue, proceed south on woods road (see New Jersey Section Six).

Trail Description, South to North

Miles	Data
0.0	From intersection of woods road near east side of ridge, proceed northwest along paved Millbrook-Blairstown Road.
0.1	Turn right off paved road, and follow woods road.
0.2	Bear left at fork in road.
0.4	Pass swamp to left of Trail. Trail descends, crosses outlet of swamp, makes sharp left turn away from road, skirting northern edge of swamp, and then curves to right.
0.6	Turn right at fork, and begin steep uphill climb.
0.7	Reach clearing for powerline, with views to left across Wallkill Valley and Pocono Plateau. Follow powerline to right across ridge for about 0.1 mile, then turn left near second powerline tower and reenter woods. (Sand Pond of Camp No-Be-Bo-Sco, Bergen Council, Boy

Scouts of America, is visible immediately below.) Trail follows crest of ridge on a relatively level path, with views to east.

2.2   After slight descent to left, reach grass-covered dirt road. Follow road for next 1.6 miles, passing several clearings.

3.1   Clearing to right of Trail provides view of Fairview Lake below.

3.5   Road to right leads about 125 feet to viewpoint overlooking northern end of Fairview Lake. Trail register is to left of Trail, 125 feet beyond road. Please sign.

3.8   Reach paved Flatbrookville Road. Trail turns right and follows paved road for 100 feet, where it turns left, crosses road, and reenters woods on footpath. Blue-blazed side trail leads to pump, a tested water source.

4.0   Cross dirt road.

5.0   Descend steeply to left of smooth rock.

5.2   Pass rock-strewn bog on right.

5.4   Cross old gravel road diagonally to right, and reenter woods. In another 300 feet, make sharp left turn, and steeply ascend face of escarpment.

5.6   One hundred fifty feet beyond top of escarpment, cross gravel road, and reach viewpoint to west. Trail joins gravel road 150 feet beyond viewpoint. Fifty feet beyond this point, blue-blazed trail to right leads 150 feet to viewpoint overlooking Crater Lake. Trail continues along gravel roads for next 1.4 miles, with occasional views of Pocono Mountains to west.

5.9   Turn left onto intersecting gravel road.

6.8   Turn left onto gravel road. One hundred twenty five feet beyond, a blue-blazed trail to left descends for 1.5 miles to Buttermilk Falls, a dependable source of water. (See description of trail at end of this section.)

7.0   Leave gravel road, and turn left on footpath into woods.

7.2   Reach viewpoint to west from open rocks.

7.8   Blue-blazed trail on left leads 75 feet to viewpoint. Trail begins to descend.

8.3   Bear right at fork, and, in another 200 feet, cross stream. Immediately past stream, blue-blazed trail to right leads 200 feet to water source. Begin climb of Rattlesnake

Mountain, soon passing through burned-out area, with views to left.

8.6   Reach rock outcrop marking summit of Rattlesnake Mountain (1,492 feet). Beautiful views to left. Begin gradual descent.

9.0   Cross short swampy area on rocks, and begin gradual ascent.

9.5   After reaching rocky, cleared area, with views through trees to right, turn right on old dirt road, and begin to descend.

9.8   Turn right off dirt road, and begin to climb, passing several rock ledges with views to left.

10.1   Reach cleared area on height of ridge. Sweeping views to the left of Wallpack Valley, and views through trees to right.

10.2   Reenter wooded area. Trail descends for 0.1 mile, then ascends slightly, and levels off.

10.5   Begin steeper descent.

10.9   Reach dirt Brink Road. (Right 0.5 mile to Lake Owassa Road; not passable by car. Left 2.5 miles to Wallpack Center; road is passable up to 0.2 mile west of Trail crossing.) **Brink Road Shelter** is 900 feet to left of Trail crossing, on right side of road. Blue-blazed trail leads to shelter and to spring 350 feet behind shelter, a dependable water source. Trail crosses road and enters woods on right, ascending gradually.

11.3   Trail levels off and follows crest of ridge.

11.4   Unmarked side trail to right leads to overlook. Four hundred feet beyond, pass field of rocks and boulders to right of Trail.

12.1   Unmarked side trail leads to overlook of Lake Owassa. Shortly afterwards, Trail climbs briefly, descends steadily, then levels off, and continues to descend moderately.

12.5   Reach Jacob's Ladder Trail, with blue-gray markings, which descends about 0.3 mile to left to junction of Coss Road and Woods Road. A.T. ascends gradually, then descends slightly, and levels off.

13.2   Reach viewpoint in large cleared area. Culver Lake and

U.S. 206 are ahead on right. Culver Fire Tower is visible straight ahead. Trail reenters woods, descends for 0.1 mile, then levels off, with several brief ascents and descents.

13.7   Reach clearing, with view of U.S. 206 to right. Trail turns right and begins steady descent.

14.0   Trail crosses gravel road, route of gold/dark-brown-blazed Acropolis Trail, and levels off for 0.2 mile, then resumes steady descent.

14.4   Turn right, leaving old woods road, and continue to descend.

14.5   Turn left onto U.S. 206.

14.6   Reach intersection of U.S. 206 and Upper North Shore Road (end of section). To continue, cross U.S. 206, and turn right on Upper North Shore Road (see New Jersey Section Four).

Buttermilk Falls Trail

This blue-blazed trail descends a vertical distance of about 1,000 feet to the base of Buttermilk Falls. The first part of the trail is quite steep, but, after about 0.3 mile, the grade moderates. A dirt road is crossed at 0.5 mile. At 1.3 miles, the trail descends very steeply for 400 feet. At the end of this descent, the top of the falls is 200 feet to the right of the trail, providing a dependable water source. The trail turns left and, after a short, steep descent at 1.6 miles, reaches Mountain Road. The base of the falls is 0.2 mile to the right along the road. Total one-way distance to top of falls is 1.5 miles; to base of falls, 1.9 miles. Allow 45 minutes for descent to top of falls; 60 minutes for return.

Millbrook-Blairstown Road to Delaware Water Gap
New Jersey Section Six
13.6 Miles

Brief Description of Section

This section follows the ridge of the Kittatinny Mountains until the Trail descends to cross the Delaware River at the Delaware Water Gap. The northern part of this section lies within the boundaries of the Delaware Water Gap National Recreation Area, while the southern part passes through Worthington State Forest. From the northern end of the section (1,260 feet), the Trail climbs to the Catfish Fire Tower (1,565 feet), then follows the Kittatinny Ridge, passing Sunfish Pond, a beautiful glacial lake. Many beautiful views can be seen along the Trail on both sides of the ridge. After descending along Dunnfield Creek, the Trail reaches the Delaware River, which it crosses on a highway bridge (350 feet).

In 1962, Congress authorized the construction of a dam across the Delaware River at Tocks Island, about five miles north of the Delaware Water Gap. This dam would have flooded much of the Wallpack Valley along the Delaware River. Several years later, the Delaware Water Gap National Recreation Area was established to provide recreational facilities at the lake that would have been created by the Tocks Island Dam. Strong opposition to the dam by conservation groups and local residents resulted in the project being repeatedly postponed. It is now highly unlikely that the Tocks Island Dam will be built, but the land acquired by the federal government for the national recreation area has provided the Trail with a protected corridor.

Toward the southern end of this section, blue- and red-blazed trails lead to the summit of Mt. Tammany (1,527 feet), which offers a magnificent view of the gap. (See description of these trails at the end of the section.)

Road Approaches

Both the northern and southern ends of this section are accessible by vehicle. At the northern end, the Trail crosses Millbrook-Blairstown Road, 6.2 miles northwest of Blairstown and 1.1 miles southeast of Millbrook Village, a collection of historic buildings. Parking is available at the Trail crossing. At the southern end, the Trail crosses the Delaware River on the I-80 toll bridge at the Delaware Water Gap. No parking is available at the Pennsylvania side of the Delaware River bridge; however, ample parking is provided at the Delaware Water Gap National Recreation Area Information Center on the New Jersey side of the bridge, 1.0 mile from the southern terminus of the section. Additional parking is available at the Dunnfield Creek Natural Area, 1.4 miles from the southern end of the section, where the Trail leaves the paved roads and begins its climb to the Kittatinny Ridge. Motorists approaching from the east should exit I-80 before crossing the bridge at the sign marked "Rest Area." Those coming from the west should take the first exit after crossing the bridge into New Jersey.

Public Transportation

Limited bus service to New York City and to other points via Martz Trailways, (800) 233-8604, is available at Delaware Water Gap, Pennsylvania, at the southern end of this section. Bus service to New York City, operated by Lakeland Bus Lines (201) 366-0600, is available in Blairstown, 6.2 miles southeast along Millbrook-Blairstown Road from the northern end of this section.

Maps

For route navigation, refer to Map Six with this guide. For area detail, refer to the following USGS 7 1/2-minute topographic quadrangles: Flatbrookville, New Jersey-Pennsylvania; Bushkill, Pennsylvania-New Jersey; Portland, New Jersey-Pennsylvania; Stroudsburg, Pennsylvania-New Jersey. Other references are NY-NJ TC Trail Maps Nos. 15 and 16 (Kittatinny Trails-South).

Shelters and Campsites

Two designated campsites are in the southern portion of this section, which passes through Worthington State Forest. *Campsite No. 1* is 0.5 mile west of the Trail, 3.0 miles from the southern end of section. *Campsite No. 2* is on the Trail, 4.6 miles from the southern end of section. No water is available at either of these campsites. In addition, a developed campground is along the Delaware River, 2.2 miles from the Trail along a woods road that leaves the Trail 4.6 miles north of the southern end of this section (fee charged for camping). Camping is prohibited in Worthington State Forest, except at these designated sites.

Camping for thru-hikers is permitted in the Delaware Water Gap National Recreation Area (from about 1.8 miles north of Sunfish Pond to the northern terminus of this section), subject to the following restrictions: Camping is permitted only in areas that are more than 0.5 mile from road accesses or the boundaries of the national recreation area. Hikers must camp not more than 100 feet from the Trail and not less than 200 feet from other campsites. Camping is prohibited within 100 feet of any stream, and any one campsite is limited to 10 persons. No open fires are permitted.

Supplies and Services

Meals, groceries, and other supplies may be obtained in the village of Delaware Water Gap, Pennsylvania (ZIP Code 18327), at the southern end of the section. Backpacking equipment and clothing, as well as repair services, are available at The Pack Shack. The Presbyterian Church of the Mountain provides an information center for hikers. At the northern end of the section, groceries, meals, a laundromat, and a post office (ZIP Code 07825) are available in Blairstown, 6.2 miles to the southeast.

Public Accommodations

Motels are available in Delaware Water Gap, Pennsylvania, at the southern end of the section, and in Blairstown, 6.2 miles southeast of the northern end of the section. The Presbyterian Church of the Mountain in Delaware Water Gap operates a hostel for hikers.

Trail Description, North to South

Miles	Data

0.0   Trail turns off paved Millbrook-Blairstown Road and continues on gravel road to south.

0.3   Road makes sharp turn to right.

0.4   Make sharp left turn off gravel road, and ascend on footpath through rhododendron thicket. Rattlesnake Spring, a dependable water source, is on left side of road, 50 feet beyond Trail turn-off. Trail follows old woods road for short distance, then turns left on footpath.

0.6   Turn left onto jeep road. In another 275 feet, turn off road, and reenter woods on footpath to right.

0.7   Turn right on jeep road, and ascend to Catfish Fire Tower.

1.0   Reach Catfish Fire Tower and small adjacent building (1,565 feet). Sixty-foot-high tower offers splendid 360-degree view. Trail reenters woods and continues on relatively level footpath, with views through trees to left.

2.0   Trail comes out at southeast side of ledge and runs for short distance along rim, with good views to left. Orange-blazed Rattlesnake Swamp Trail goes off to right and leads in about 0.5 mile to Catfish Pond.

2.1   Trail comes out on rim for second time.

2.7   Begin descent to Mohican Road.

3.3   Cross dirt Mohican Road, and reenter woods to left. In another 50 feet, cross stream, a water source, and begin to ascend, often steeply.

3.6   Reach end of steep section. Trail continues to ascend on moderate grade.

4.8   View to left of Trail of storage ponds for hydroelectric development.

5.3   Reach old, grass-grown Kaiser Road, which comes in from right. Continue ahead on old road.

5.5   Turn right off woods road, and continue on footpath, with views to right. (Road descends mountain to south-east, with spring 0.3 mile down slope.)

5.8   Enter Worthington State Forest.

6.0   Reach viewpoint. To left are storage ponds for Yards Creek pumped-storage hydroelectric development. Delaware River is visible to right. Directly behind, Catfish Fire Tower may be visible between ridges.

6.1   Powerline crosses Trail, with views on both sides of ridge.

6.3   View west (over trees) toward Pennsylvania at open area. Trail begins to descend.

6.7   Cross brook, and begin to ascend.

7.4   Turn right at double blaze.

7.6   Blue-blazed trail to right leads 600 feet to spring, a water source.

7.7   Reach eastern end of Sunfish Pond. No camping permitted near pond. Trail continues along shore of pond on rocky footpath.

8.1   Cross outlet of pond.

8.4   Reach western end of Sunfish Pond. Note monument to right of Trail designating the Sunfish Pond Natural Area as a registered national landmark. Continue along woods road.

9.0   Reach **Campsite No. 2** (no water). Turn left off woods road, and continue on footpath. Road straight ahead, which is blue-blazed Douglas Trail, leads 2.2 miles to developed **campground** in Worthington State Forest along Delaware River.

10.6   After passing through burned-out area (now starting to regenerate), reach trail junction. Yellow-blazed Beulahland Trail to right leads to **Campsite No. 1** in 0.5 mile (no water), and Farview Parking Area on River Road in 1.0 mile. Unmarked trail to left leads 0.2 mile to Holly Spring, a water source (may fail in dry weather), and continues to headwaters of Dunnfield Creek. A.T. continues straight ahead, descending gradually.

11.7   Blue-blazed trail coming in from left leads to Mt. Tammany. (See description, page 166.) A.T. continues along right bank of Dunnfield Creek, still descending.

12.0	Turn left off woods road, and, in 200 feet, cross wooden bridge over Dunnfield Creek.
12.1	Reach parking area and pump, a tested water source. Trail continues through parking area.
12.2	At end of parking area, turn left along paved road. Continue along road for 250 feet, then make right turn at underpass and go under I-80. (Red-blazed trail to Mt. Tammany begins at parking area straight ahead on paved road. See description at end of section.)
12.3	At other side of underpass, turn right, and continue along paved road parallel to I-80.
12.6	Pass trail register (please sign) and Delaware Water Gap National Recreation Area Information Center (water, restrooms, picnic area, boat launching, and parking). Continue along paved road.
12.9	Cross bridge over Delaware River into Pennsylvania.
13.6	Section ends where chained-off street comes in from left before toll plaza. To continue, turn left onto chained-off street. Description of A.T. continues in the *Appalachian Trail Guide to Pennsylvania*.

Trail Description, South to North

Miles   **Data**

0.0	Turn right at end of chained-off street onto sidewalk along I-80, and cross bridge over Delaware River.
0.7	After crossing bridge, continue along service road, which parallels I-80.
1.0	Pass trail register (please sign) and Delaware Water Gap National Recreation Area Information Center (water, restrooms, picnic area, boat launching, and parking). Continue along paved road parallel to I-80.
1.3	Turn left at underpass, and go under I-80. Make left turn at other side of underpass, and continue along paved road for about 250 feet. (Red-blazed trail to Mt. Tammany begins at parking area to right of underpass. See description at end of section.)

1.4   Turn right into parking area at sign, "Dunnfield Creek Natural Area." Trail continues through parking area.

1.5   Pass pump, a tested water source. Trail leaves parking area and enters woods.

1.6   Turn left, and cross wooden bridge over Dunnfield Creek. Two hundred feet past bridge, Trail turns right on woods road and continues along left bank of Dunnfield Creek.

1.9   Take left fork, and continue on woods road. Blue-blazed trail to right leads to Mt. Tammany. (See description at end of section.) Continue gradual ascent toward Sunfish Pond.

3.0   Reach trail junction. To left, yellow-blazed Beulahland Trail leads to **Campsite No. 1** in 0.5 mile (no water), and Farview Parking Area on River Road in 1.0 mile. To right, unmarked trail leads 0.2 mile to Holly Spring, a water source (may fail in very dry weather), and continues to headwaters of Dunnfield Creek. A.T. continues, with area burned out several years ago (now starting to regenerate) noticeable to right of Trail. Ridge of Kittatinny Mountains is also visible to right of Trail.

4.6   Reach **Campsite No. 2** (no water) at junction with woods road. Trail turns right on road. Road to left (blue-blazed Douglas Trail) leads 2.2 miles to developed **campground** in Worthington State Forest along Delaware River.

5.2   Reach Sunfish Pond. Note monument on left of Trail designating Sunfish Pond Natural Area as a registered national landmark. No camping permitted near pond. Trail continues along left shore of pond.

5.5   Cross outlet of pond. In another 350 feet, turn right at double blaze.

5.9   Pass east end of pond.

6.0   Blue-blazed trail to left leads 600 feet to spring, a water source.

6.2   Turn left at double blaze. Shortly afterwards, start descent to brook.

6.9   Cross brook.

7.3   View west (over trees) toward Pennsylvania at open area.

7.3   Powerline crosses Trail. Views on both sides of ridge.

7.6   Reach crest of ridge. To right, note storage ponds for Yards Creek pumped-storage hydroelectric development. Delaware River is visible to left. Directly ahead, Catfish Fire Tower may be visible between ridges.

7.8   Leave Worthington State Forest, and enter Delaware Water Gap National Recreation Area.

8.1   Reach old grass-grown Kaiser Road. (To right, road descends mountain to southeast. Spring is 0.3 mile down slope.) Continue ahead on old road.

8.3   Take right fork of trail. Kaiser Road continues to left, leading to old copper mines.

8.8   View to right of Trail of storage ponds for hydroelectric development.

9.3   Trail turns left at double blaze.

10.0   Start steeper descent to Mohican Road.

10.3   Cross stream, a source of water, then immediately cross dirt Mohican Road. Trail reenters woods to left and begins ascent of Kittatinny Ridge.

10.9   Reach top of ridge, with views along Trail to right.

11.5   Trail comes out on southeast side of ledge and runs for short distance along rim, with good views to right.

11.6   Trail comes out on rim for second time. Orange-blazed Rattlesnake Swamp Trail goes off to left and leads in about 0.5 mile to Catfish Pond.

12.6   Reach Catfish Fire Tower (and small adjacent building). Sixty-foot-high tower offers splendid 360-degree view. Begin descent to Millbrook-Blairstown Road along jeep road.

12.9   Leave jeep road, and follow footpath to left.

13.0   Turn left on jeep road for 275 feet, then turn off road, and reenter woods on footpath to right.

13.2   Turn right on old woods road at powerline. Pass through rhododendron thicket, then turn right onto gravel road. Fifty feet to left on road is Rattlesnake Spring, a dependable water source.

13.4   Road makes sharp turn to left.

13.6   Reach paved Millbrook-Blairstown Road (end of section). To continue, turn left along road (see New Jersey Section Five).

Mt. Tammany Trails

Two side trails lead from the A.T. to the summit of Mt. Tammany, from which there are splendid views over the Delaware Water Gap and west into Pennsylvania.

The red-blazed River Ridge Trail begins at the parking area near the I-80 underpass, 1.3 miles from the southern end of the section. It ascends steadily but at a moderate rate, except for one short, steep climb. The blue-blazed Mt. Tammany Trail turns off the A.T. 1.9 miles from the southern end of the section, crosses Dunnfield Creek, and ascends gradually to the summit. Both trails join at the summit and can be combined to make a scenic loop.

Table of Distances

Miles			Miles	
Sec.	Cum.		Cum.	Sec.

N.Y. Section 2

0.0	0.0	Hoyt Road	163.6	7.0
0.9	0.9	Duell Hollow Road	162.7	6.1
1.1	1.1	Wiley (Webatuck) Shelter	162.5	5.9
1.5	1.5	Leather Hill Road	162.1	5.5
6.5	6.5	Old N.Y. 22	157.1	0.5
7.0	7.0	N.Y. 22	156.6	0.0

N.Y. Section 3

0.0	7.0	N.Y. 22	156.6	7.0
2.4	9.4	County 20	154.2	4.6
3.1	10.1	Telephone Pioneers Shelter	153.5	3.9
3.4	10.4	West Mountain	153.2	3.6
3.9	10.9	Penny Road	152.7	3.1
7.0	14.0	N.Y. 55	149.6	0.0

N.Y. Section 4

0.0	14.0	N.Y. 55	149.6	7.1
0.2	14.2	Old N.Y. 55	149.4	6.9
2.1	16.1	Depot Hill Road	147.5	5.0
3.4	17.4	Morgan Stewart Shelter	146.2	3.7

3.5	17.5	Mt. Egbert	146.1	3.6
5.7	19.7	I-84 Overpass	143.9	1.4
7.1	21.1	N.Y. 52	142.5	0.0

N.Y. Section 5

0.0	21.1	N.Y. 52	142.5	4.7
1.5	22.6	Hosner Mountain Road	141.0	3.2
1.8	22.9	Trail to Bailey Spring Campsites	140.7	2.9
4.7	25.8	Taconic State Parkway	137.8	0.0

N.Y. Section 6

0.0	25.8	Taconic State Parkway	137.8	7.3
0.4	26.2	Hortontown Road, RPH Cabin	137.4	6.9
2.7	28.5	Long Hill Road	135.1	4.6
3.1	28.9	Shenandoah Mountain	134.7	4.2
7.3	33.1	N.Y. 301	130.5	0.0

N.Y. Section 7

0.0	33.1	N.Y. 301	130.5	7.5
2.2	35.3	Sunk Mine Road	128.3	5.3
3.7	36.8	Dennytown Road	126.8	3.8
7.5	40.6	Canopus Hill Road	123.0	0.0

N.Y. Section 8

0.0	40.6	Canopus Hill Road	123.0	5.0
0.7	41.3	Canopus Hill	122.3	4.3
1.7	42.3	Chapman Road	121.3	3.3
2.5	43.1	Denning Hill	120.5	2.5
4.4	45.0	Old West Point Road	118.6	0.6
5.0	45.6	U.S. 9	118.0	0.0

N.Y. Section 9

0.0	45.6	U.S. 9	118.0	5.8
3.3	48.9	South Mountain Pass	114.7	2.5
3.5	49.1	Hemlock Springs Campsite	114.5	2.3
5.0	50.6	N.Y. 9D	113.0	0.8
5.8	51.4	Bear Mountain Bridge	112.2	0.0

N.Y. Section 10

0.0	51.4	Bear Mountain Bridge	112.2	13.3
0.8	52.2	Bear Mountain Inn	111.4	12.5
2.6	54.0	Bear Mountain	109.6	10.7
4.2	55.6	Seven Lakes Drive	108.0	9.1
5.8	57.2	Trail to West Mountain Shelter	106.4	7.5
7.0	58.4	Palisades Interstate Parkway	105.2	6.3
7.7	59.1	Black Mountain	104.5	5.6
9.1	60.5	Brien Memorial Shelter	103.1	4.2
11.1	62.5	Seven Lakes Drive	101.1	2.2
13.3	64.7	Arden Valley Road	98.9	0.0

N.Y. Section 11

0.0	64.7	Arden Valley Road	98.9	7.5
1.0	65.7	Fingerboard Shelter	97.9	6.5
3.2	67.9	Lemon Squeezer	95.7	4.3
7.5	72.2	N.Y. 17	91.4	0.0

N.Y. Section 12

0.0	72.2	N.Y. 17	91.4	11.9
1.1	73.3	Arden Mountain	90.3	10.8
1.8	74.0	Orange Turnpike	89.6	10.1
3.2	75.4	East Mombasha Road	88.2	8.7

4.9	77.1	West Mombasha Road	86.5	7.0
6.0	78.2	Mombasha High Road	85.4	5.9
8.0	80.2	Fitzgerald Falls	83.4	3.9
8.3	80.5	Lakes Road	83.1	3.6
10.1	82.3	Cat Rocks	81.3	1.8
10.6	82.8	Eastern Pinnacles	80.8	1.3
11.9	84.1	N.Y. 17A	79.5	0.0

N.Y. Section 13

0.0	84.1	N.Y. 17A	79.5	5.9
5.4	89.5	Prospect Rock	74.1	0.5
5.9	90.0	State Line Trail	73.6	0.0

N.J. Section 1

0.0	90.0	State Line Trail	73.6	10.1
1.1	91.1	Long House Creek	72.5	9.0
2.2	92.2	Long House Road	71.4	7.9
3.6	93.6	Warwick Turnpike	70.0	6.5
4.1	94.1	Campsite	69.5	6.0
4.2	94.2	Wawayanda Road	69.4	5.9
5.1	95.1	Iron Mountain Road Bridge	68.5	5.0
6.5	96.5	Barrett Road	67.1	3.6
8.9	98.9	Wawayanda Mountain	64.7	1.2
10.1	100.1	N.J. 94	63.5	0.0

N.J. Section 2

0.0	100.1	N.J. 94	63.5	11.1
1.7	101.8	County 517	61.0	8.6
4.1	104.2	County 565	59.4	7.0
5.3	105.4	Pochuck Mountain	58.2	5.8
7.3	107.4	Wallkill Road	56.2	3.8

| 9.6 | 109.7 | Wallkill River | 53.9 | 1.5 |
| 11.1 | 111.2 | N.J. 284 | 52.4 | 0.0 |

N.J. Section 3

0.0	111.2	N.J. 284	52.4	9.9
1.0	112.2	Lott Road	51.4	8.9
2.0	113.2	Unionville Road	50.4	7.9
3.3	114.5	Goodrich Road	49.1	6.6
4.3	115.5	Gemmer Road	48.1	5.6
6.1	117.3	Courtwright Road	46.3	3.8
6.9	118.1	County 519	45.5	3.0
8.2	119.4	High Point Shelter	44.2	1.7
9.9	121.1	N.J. 23	42.5	0.0

N.J. Section 4

0.0	121.1	N.J. 23	42.5	14.3
2.5	123.6	Trail to Rutherford Shelter	40.0	11.8
5.3	126.4	Deckertown Turnpike	37.2	9.0
5.5	126.6	Mashipacong Shelter	37.0	8.8
8.0	129.1	Crigger Road	34.5	6.3
8.9	130.0	Sunrise Mountain	33.6	5.4
11.2	132.3	Trail to Gren Anderson Shelter	31.3	3.1
12.3	133.4	Culver Fire Tower	30.2	2.0
14.3	135.4	U.S. 206	28.2	0.0

N.J. Section 5

0.0	135.4	U.S. 206	28.2	14.6
3.7	139.1	Brink Road Shelter	24.5	10.9
6.0	141.4	Rattlesnake Mountain	22.2	8.6
7.8	143.2	Trail to Buttermilk Falls	20.4	6.8
10.8	146.2	Flatbrookville Road	17.4	3.8

| 14.6 | 150.0 | Millbrook-Blairstown Road | 13.6 | 0.0 |

N.J. Section 6

0.0	150.0	Millbrook-Blairstown Road	13.6	13.6
1.0	151.0	Catfish Fire Tower	12.6	12.6
3.3	153.3	Mohican Road	10.3	10.3
7.7	157.7	Sunfish Pond	5.2	5.2
9.0	159.0	Campsite No. 2	4.6	4.6
10.6	160.6	Trail to Campsite No. 1	3.0	3.0
12.2	162.2	Dunnfield Creek Parking Area	1.4	1.4
13.6	163.6	Delaware Water Gap, Pa.	0.0	0.0

Index

Guidebook Contributors

Daniel D. Chazin, Editor
Dave Bieri
Walter and Jane Daniels
Richard J. Kavalek
Elizabeth D. Levers
Anne Lutkenhouse
Ron Rosen
George Schelling
Norm Sills